T0386655

MALTA

Hardie Grant

BOOKS

To Linda, Max and Leon, my ancestors
and the people of Malta.

MALTA

SIMON

BAJADA

Mediterranean recipes from the islands

FOREWORD

By Pippa Mattei and Julia Busuttil Nishimura

In 1698, a Russian traveller to Malta records that in Valletta ... *there were many shops and wares of all kinds, and that there was bread and food stuffs of all kinds and many fruits too, and food was not expensive.*

The Maltese islands, located between North Africa and Southern Italy, are blessed with sheltered harbours, bays and creeks. For centuries, the role of Malta in recorded history is that of haven and crossroads, to be conquered for strategic purposes. Thus, it became a pit stop of sorts for seafaring merchants, and with the arrival of the Knights Hospitallers from Rhodes, Malta's maritime role enhanced further, to become an important Mediterranean base, which continued until the mid 20th century.

It would transpire that most Maltese dishes are a curious amalgam of trade, colonial influence and local produce, dating back much further than one might imagine. Apiaries dating back to Roman times can be found here, and we can boast of coffee and chocolate being consumed in Malta in the mid 1600s, which would explain how we come to have a festive recipe for chestnuts in spiced hot chocolate and sweetened with sugar, known as *Imbuljuta*, still served on Christmas Eve after midnight mass.

Over the centuries, the recipes and produce of Malta have sustained us and kept us alive, even during times of scarcity, such as when under siege during WWII. Our connection to the past can be better understood through the meals that we continue to enjoy today.

Walking through a village street in Malta or Gozo, one is bound to pick up the wonderful aromas wafting out of our homes and bakeries, where the preparation of some meal is underway – a simmering vegetable *minestra*, a vibrant fish *aljotta* soup, the baking of ricotta-filled pastries called *qassatat*, and of course the unmistakable smell of the Maltese *ħobża* rising in the wood-fired oven of the village bakery, located a few steps from the parish church.

All this whetting of the appetite for a typical Maltese meal, cooked with care, using the freshest ingredients bought a few hours earlier from the vegetable truck, the fishmonger or the village baker!

For anyone who grew up in Malta, the connection between food, family and fond memories is strong. Who can forget snacking on wonderful *ħobż biż-żejt* after a refreshing swim in the sparkling Mediterranean, downed with aniseed-laced coffee, kept hot in a flask? Or fighting over the crunchy top of the *imqarrun*, baked macaroni that is a staple at every large family gathering?

Despite a waning of traditional food preparation over recent years, due to frenetic lifestyles and the proliferation of supermarket meals, there is a renewed interest in our kitchen and the sourcing of ingredients, akin with current international trends. We are finding time to reconnect with our traditions and delve into our culinary lore, and, most excitingly, we are giving these centuries-old recipes a new lease of life.

In this compendium of recipes, Simon brings a freshness to many tried and tested recipes; he has captured the essence of our Maltese cuisine to take it beyond our shores, where it might arouse the interest of the inquisitive cook, who through these pages will discover that Maltese food is indeed the 'caper' of the Mediterranean diet.

Perhaps the reader will be enticed to make the journey to our islands where they can enjoy first hand not only the fare from our fields and kitchens, but also the diverse history and warm hospitality of the Maltese people.

Pippa Mattei, Maltese cook and author

As a proud daughter of Maltese immigrants, recipes such as the ones in this book are incredibly special and sentimental to me. I am often asked 'What actually is Maltese food?' The country's cuisine is mysterious to many, but it's the thread that connects us to our culture. It has also fostered my lifelong love for ingredients such as broad beans, capers, ricotta and rabbit to name a few. Simon's work is such a generous gift to us all – a wonderful body of work which beautifully illustrates what Maltese food really is.

My fondest childhood memories are centered around the Maltese kitchen. The kitchen was a place of learning and growth, and almost like a classroom. Recipes such as Simon's *Gozitan Ravioli* – bulging with *irkotta* and covered in *zalza* – is something my dad would prepare on a Saturday for lunch. We would walk to our local beach and collect sea water to make the cheese, and I can still see the colourful plastic baskets sitting on the sink with the steaming curds.

Reading *Malta* transported me to our back porch step, podding bags of broad beans with my nanna to dry and make *Bigilla*. It's where my aunty taught me how to make *Timpana*, and my cousin taught me how to break down a rabbit for *Stuffat tal-fenek* and stuff marrows for *Qarabaghli mimli fil-forn*, just as you find in this book. If there was a food that defined my youth, it is *ħobż biż-żejt*, which I ate as my packed lunch or an after school snack. These foods have always felt like a gateway to Maltese culture, heritage and family and reading about them has been life-enhancing and rather moving.

Cooking Maltese food with my own children is now the best way to bring my treasured culture into our home. We prepare *Figolli* or *Kwarezimal* every Easter with my mum, celebrate Maltese Independence Day with a long lunch and often spend Saturdays making *Ravjul*. I remember the moment I arrived in Malta for the first time as a teenager – I felt like I had come home. Reading Simon's book alongside his stunning photography has taken me home too. This book will prove to be an indispensable bible in my kitchen, and is a glorious representation of Malta and its rich and diverse food. Prosit!

Julia Busuttil Nishimura, Australian cook and author

CONTENTS

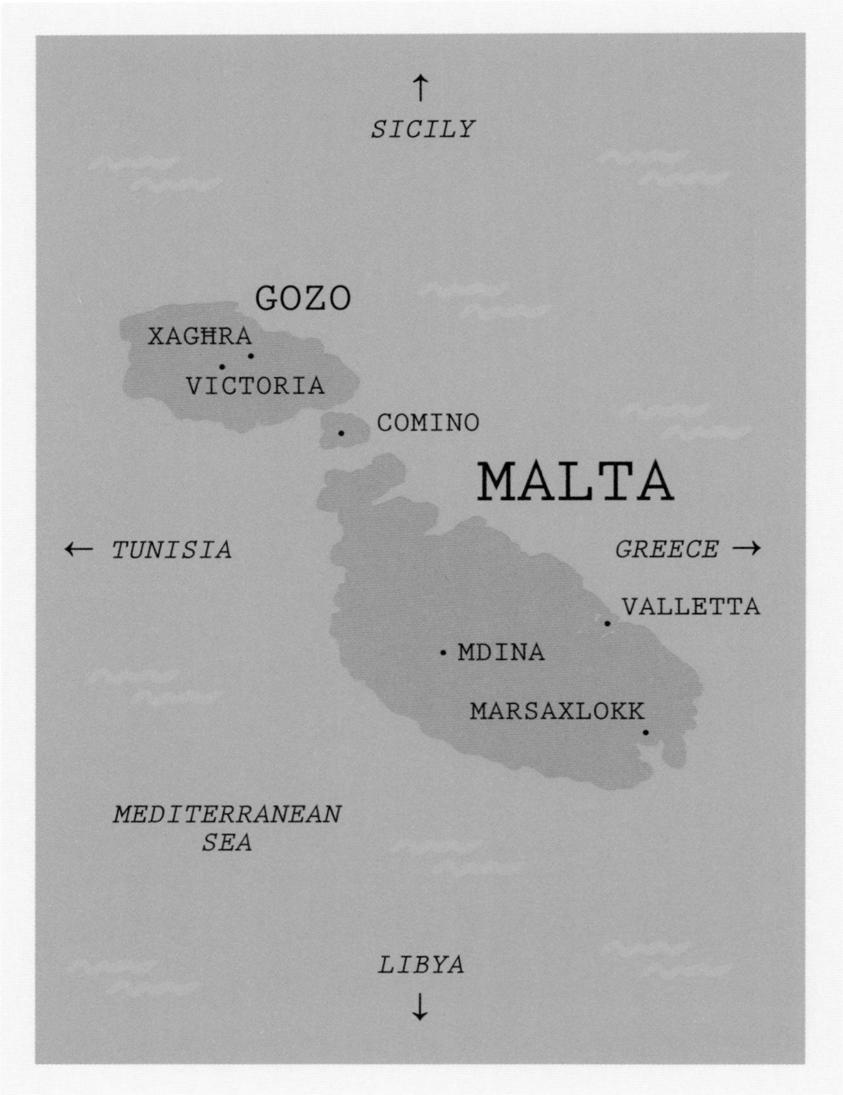

SICILY ↑

GOZO

XAGĦRA

VICTORIA

COMINO

MALTA

← TUNISIA

GREECE →

VALLETTA

• MDINA

MARSAXLOKK

MEDITERRANEAN
SEA

LIBYA
↓

INTRODUCTION

In perfect harmony, the Maltese cuisine balances raw agrarian produce, fruits of the sea, and honed yet simple techniques, with extra zest garnered by the spoils of the islands' geography.

Malta sits south of Sicily and east of Tunisia – limestone rocks protruding out of the Mediterranean Sea on the African tectonic plate. It's the world's tenth smallest country, with a main island that is just 27 kilometres long. One can drive top to bottom in under an hour.

To the north is the smaller island of Gozo with its capital, Victoria. Gozo is less densely inhabited, more agricultural; its people are known as Gozitans. The climate is Mediterranean with hot summers, mild winters and some rainfall in autumn and winter. The archipelago is a stunning collection of sheltered bays with transparent blue waters around every corner.

Over the centuries, many cultures have left something behind in the Maltese kitchen. Families living on this outcrop of the Mediterranean have had their say in what goes and what stays. The influences have steeped together to create a unique flavour profile formed over many occupations. I'd argue that this presents us with the most intriguing 'minestrone' of Mediterranean cuisine.

In perfect harmony, the Maltese cuisine balances raw agrarian produce, fruits of the sea, and honed yet simple techniques, with extra zest garnered by the spoils of the islands' geography. Malta's closest neighbour, the island of Sicily, has influenced the cuisine the most, with Malta becoming an extension of Sicily for over four hundred years. But North Africa, Greece and wider Italy have also added to the mix.

After the Kingdom of Sicily came the Knights of Malta. Needing a new base, this Catholic and military order was granted control of the country in the 16th century. These knights had long dedicated themselves to caring for sick and poor pilgrims. A mix of cultures unto themselves, the men had grandiose tastes, and added plenty of fine fare to the pot.

The French occupied Malta briefly at the end of the 18th century, but the English spent over 150 years on the island and left a clear mark. Ingredients such as cheddar and corned beef crept into traditional recipes, sometimes clashing with their Mediterranean roots. But every influence has had its positives, giving Maltese cuisine many points of difference.

Put simply, defining an exact genetic make-up of Maltese food is no easy task, and likely fraught with anomalies. (Although the timeline on pages 18 and 19 will give you some historical insight.) The origins of the peppered cheeselet (ġbejniet tal-bżar) on page 47 is a great example of many possible conundrums, as it resembles cheeses you might find in a food market of provincial France, but is also strikingly similar to shanklish from a store in Aleppo, Syria. Polarities are not limited to food; Malta's Semitic language is derived from Siculo-Arabic (or Sicilian Arabic, a language that is now extinct), and Catholic worshippers pray to Alla, the Maltese name for God.

Malta is home to some of the oldest surviving structures in the world – ancient limestone temples strewn across Malta and Gozo, predating the pyramids of Giza. On Xagħra in the middle of Gozo, the Ġgantija megalithic temples date back to 3600 BCE. Gozitan legend has it they were built by a giantess who ate only broad beans and honey.

The people of Malta have much experience looking outwards. The geography of the surrounding sea and the placement between Africa, Europe and the East have made Malta forever a port nation. Exotic produce has passed through for centuries, with everything from vanilla beans to African gazelles cited in old recipes. The Maltese have always had a boldness to try new foods, and were amongst the first Europeans to eat chocolate and drink coffee. It is said that Malta, along with Spain and southern Italy, was one of the earliest adopters of tomatoes, once widely considered to be poisonous. Tomatoes have such a stronghold in the cuisine today, and the Maltese have an unabashed love for kunserva, the islands' own rich tomato paste.

Local place names hint at ingredients, such as the island of Comino between the mainland and Gozo, named after the wild cumin found growing there, and Filfla, a small rocky outcrop to the south whose name is derived from 'felfel', Arabic for chilli. The Greeks and Romans once referred to Malta as Melite, thought to be from the Greek word for honey. The honey of Malta was renowned then as it is today, particularly the honey made from wild thyme in summer.

In spring on the lofty cliffs of Gozo, villagers gather wild caper buds for preservation before they burst into beautiful white and violet blooms. Wild herbs growing on the limestone take on a deep flavour as poor soil stunts their growth and the hot sun has an intensifying effect.

At the markets you can find the staple spread of Mediterranean vegetables, including locally grown tomatoes, broad beans, potatoes, cabbages, artichokes, kohlrabi and the popular round zucchini (courgettes) called marrows. There is also interesting produce that pops up for a few weeks of the year, such as freshly harvested chickpeas that children like to snack on, or medlars for making jam or fruit wine.

With the peasant roots of Maltese cuisine, vegetables are consumed more than any other food group, not merely as accompaniments, but often dishes in their own right. Yes, we hear most of braised rabbit, timpana (a bolognese pasta pie of sorts, page 161) and bragioli (beef olives, page 156) – the Maltese dishes that are famed for their novelty and often cooked on weekends or special occasions. But it's the everyday food of Malta, alongside these classics, that I want to share with you in this book. The recipes will show you the traditional dishes that have come to be loved and have lasted the centuries, as well as new interpretations using the islands' ingredients.

The Maltese are adaptable in nature, a result of hosting visitors through millennia. But in the tourism boom of late last century, a few too many restaurants catered for the tourist with fish and chips and hamburgers. Thankfully this is changing. Maltese food is growing in diversity, with chefs putting forward their classics, owning their cuisine, and insisting visitors savour its worth. With Malta's relatively recent independence and new-found interest in its own dishes, it's exciting to think of what is still to come.

AUTHOR'S NOTE

Aside from my immediate family, I've often been the only Bajada in the places I've lived, yet in Malta, my family name is common. Locals immediately recognise my heritage as Maltese. Driving in the streets of the small cities, I feel 'at home'. Familiarity abounds with a dry, dusty climate and Catholic symbolism dotted everywhere, just like in Adelaide where I was raised. Recognisable surnames are sprawled across signs – the same names of many children I went to school with in Australia, but which I never knew as Maltese.

There are just 500 000 people living on the archipelago, but the Maltese diaspora is strong around the world. Australia is home to over 200 000 people of Maltese heritage, with smaller populations in the United States, Canada and England. It's almost a given that anyone you meet in Malta has a relative living abroad, and broaching the subject always leads to a friendly conversation.

When I mentioned my last name to a woman running her vegetable stall at Qormi Market, she remarked 'But you have Maltese blood,' cutting me off as I tried to tell her I grew up in Australia. She even told me about the Gozitan village where the Bajada family name is thought to have originated – Xagħra, in the middle of Gozo. Some generations back, my ancestors and many other Maltese up and left Gozo to capitalise on their shipping skills in other parts of the world.

While documenting the dying craft of home-produced *ilma żahar* (orange-blossom water) in Xagħra, I sat opposite Lawrence Bajada, who is no direct relation. He explained to me the process of picking the blossoms and the distillation, then we tasted the result. His mannerisms and features were so similar to my late grandfather's that the nostalgia was overwhelming. I thought to myself, there is no arguing with the woman from the market!

I feel very fortunate for the opportunity to dive into the culture of Malta and connect with my heritage in writing this book. The recipe collection ahead is not intended to be 'the be all and end all' of Maltese cuisine (there are plenty more dishes). Through sharing my favourite dishes, those I feel are uniquely Maltese and hold a place in the hearts of those living on the islands, my goal has been to inspire the Maltese diaspora living abroad to bring more Maltese cuisine into their kitchen. Maybe that's you, enjoy the cooking!

MALTA THROUGH HISTORY

This timeline illustrates some of the social and political history of Malta, and how it has influenced the cuisine. With peasant and agricultural beginnings, the food was based on products such as wheat and vegetables, then each phase in history added another layer. For example, the Phoenicians brought fishing skills, the Arabs introduced citrus, the Knights of Malta brought an appreciation for fine foods such as saffron and ice cream, and during the years of the English, some of Malta's pastry recipes developed.

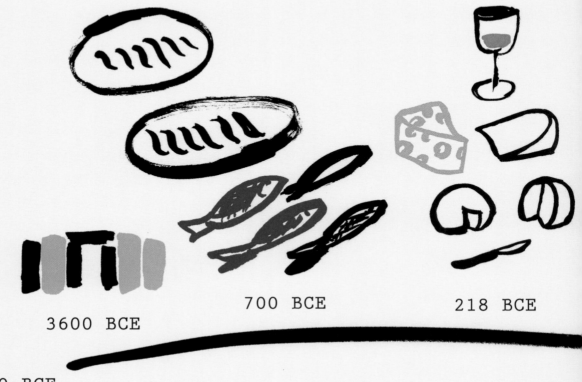

700 BCE

218 BCE

3600 BCE

5900 BCE

5900 BCE The islands of Malta are first inhabited, with people arriving from the Mediterranean, Europe and Africa.

3600 BCE The first of the Ggantija temples is built on Gozo. Malta's Neolithic civilisation disappears around 2500 BCE, but new people of the Bronze Age begin migrating to the islands soon afterwards.

700 BCE Malta is colonised by the Phoenicians, who hail from modern-day Lebanon. They are master seafarers and fishermen and introduce rabbits, olives, bread and wine.

218 BCE Roman rule begins, merging into the Byzantine (or Eastern Roman) Empire over 600 years later. Cheese, honey and wine are some of the well-known foods of the era.

870 The Aghlabids, an Arab dynasty, expel the Byzantines and bring spices, citrus and figs, as well as terraced fields and the waterwheel.

1091 Sicily takes control. There are many changes of power within the Kingdom of Sicily over the next four hundred years, from Norman to German to French to Spanish sparking a turning point in modern Maltese history.

870   1530   1800   1964

1530 The Knights of Malta, also known as the Order of Saint John, are given rights to rule Malta. They reinforce Christianity in the country, and bring regional dishes and food preparation techniques from France and Italy. Malta begins importing foreign delights such as ice to make ice cream, coffee, chocolate and exotic fruit.

1565 The Ottoman Empire attempts to invade but is famously repelled by the knights.

1798 The French attack under Napoleon Bonaparte and the knights surrender.

1800 The Maltese rebel, ousting the French with the help of the British. Malta officially becomes a colony of Britain in 1813. Roast meat meals, custard, sponge cakes and puddings are soon to be staples in many households.

1919 Limited imports and the rising cost of living (notably the price of flour) after World War I incite riots. Four people are killed by British soldiers sparking a turning point in modern Maltese history.

1964 Malta is granted independence from Britain but remains part of the Commonwealth.

MALTESE COOKING

The joy of Maltese cuisine is that it's not so exact. It allows us to relinquish the dogmatic methods we might be accustomed to in some other Mediterranean cookery.

When prepared with quality produce, patience and love, Maltese cuisine most certainly delivers. It makes you appreciate the basics: tomatoes, olive oil, pasta, seafood and vegetables. Something our overstimulated appetites can benefit from. I want you to return to these recipes, hoping your book develops wear and tear, smears of tomato paste across the pages, and dried mint collected in the spine!

The joy of Maltese cuisine is that it's not so exact. Maltese food allows us to relinquish the dogmatic methods we might be accustomed to in some other Mediterranean cookery, and inject a little of our own taste into the dishes. One thing Maltese families agree on is there is no exact way to make *ross il-forn* or bread pudding, as everyone has their own take on the basic idea.

At times, Maltese dishes repeat themselves. The sauces of stews such as rabbit or *lampuki* are served on top of pasta as an entree, and stews are also made into pies. Vermicelli pie and baked macaroni reinvent pasta – recipes that have likely come about from leftover food after the monstrous event that is the Maltese family weekend lunch.

Maltese cuisine is not full of fancy kitchen skills. One notable technique is long, slow cooking, as food was historically cooked next to or over a fire in earthenware pots. Then later the *kenur* was eventually replaced by tabletop kerosene cookers called *kuciniera*. The home cook would prepare the day's lunch by filling a pot early in the morning and leaving it to simmer while in the field. This practice is almost extinct now, and so too the novel concept of families taking vessels of food to their corner baker on weekends to cook in the stone oven. For this type of cooking, I suggest using a cast-iron pot on your stovetop. If you enjoy *ġbejniet* cheese, then it would be worth finding a set of small cheese baskets called *qwieleb* online.

Maltese cuisine shines the light on quality produce – simple fare with ingredients that are grown and cooked well, coming together to make the perceivably mundane glorious. For this reason, I recommend using the best produce you can find (organic when possible), and don't forget to sample as you go, always checking your seasoning. (Zucchini without salt is not zucchini at all!)

Onions, garlic and tomato sautéed in olive oil form the basis of many dishes. I can smell this as I write it, and know the importance of quality tomatoes. In summer, I encourage you to use fresh ripe tomatoes, which makes your cooking more sprightly and sweet. The technique I use to prepare them is to score the bottom with two incisions to create an 'X'. This end of the tomato is then grated on the rough side of a box grater, and the result is a fresh purée with only the skin of the tomato left behind. The skin acts as hand protection against the sharp edges of the grater. With a little practice, the technique is quick and easy. One caveat though – a lot of juice runs from the tomatoes, so use a lipped tray or wide bowl. In winter when tomatoes are out of season, use high-quality tinned tomatoes. For all recipes in this book that include ricotta, use soft ricotta (like a paste) rather than drained ricotta. If you can't find soft ricotta, mash up drained ricotta with some teaspoons of milk until it becomes paste-like.

The oven temperatures given in this book are for fan-forced ovens. Please increase the temperature by approximately 15°C (30°F) if using an oven without a fan.

THE MEDITERRANEAN PANTRY

Maltese cuisine is classically Mediterranean and features flavours you may already be familiar with, but there are some twists and surprises. Here are the key ingredients that are fundamental to the Maltese kitchen.

BROAD BEANS
Abundant in spring, the fresh beans make their way into some classic Maltese recipes. Dried split broad (fava) beans called *favetta* are also used in soup.

CAPERS
Found wild all over the islands. Buds are picked from the bushes before blooming and are preserved in salt and vinegar.

CAROB
Native to the Mediterranean, this tree handles the dry climate of Malta. The sweet beans inside the brown pods are made into a syrup used in desserts, which is also drunk for its health properties.

CITRUS: FRUIT, ZEST AND BLOSSOM WATER
Citrus trees are at home in Malta, and the islands' blood oranges were prized in Europe in the 18th century. Zest is commonly used in recipes.

CRUSTY WHITE BREAD
The loaf known as *ħobż* and its flatter, ring-shaped sibling called *ftira* are an integral part of Maltese cuisine. Seldom are any other breads eaten in Malta.

HERBS, PARTICULARLY MINT AND PARSLEY
Others used are marjoram, oregano, thyme and basil.

HONEY
Maltese honey takes on different flavours through the seasons. Spring yields a floral honey followed by one flavoured by wild thyme in the summer months, and in autumn a deeper flavour is characterised by carob and eucalyptus. It's a treasured ingredient used in sweets and for remedial purposes.

MIXED SPICE
Found in many Maltese sweets; I call it Christmas spice because the combination of cinnamon, ground coriander, nutmeg, ginger, cloves and allspice is so distinctly related to Christmas.

OLIVES
Present on Malta for millennia and thriving in the Maltese soil and climate. The cities of Żebbuġ (also the name of a village on Gozo) and Żejtun translate as 'olive' in Maltese and Arabic.

PASTA
Small bead shapes known as *kusksu* are common, as well as penne, macaroni and spaghetti.

PRICKLY PEAR
Introduced but growing abundantly in the Maltese conditions. The plant can be found on the edge of farms acting as a windbreak, and is used for its fruit. Malta's most popular duty-free purchase is a liqueur called *bajtra* made from prickly pear.

RABBIT
Once wild (though introduced), and now farmed due to its popularity. There is even a seasoning mix in Malta called rabbit spice.

RICOTTA (IRKOTTA)
Mild and creamy Maltese ricotta differs from Italian ricotta in that it is not produced from whey. It is used in traditional dishes such as *qassatat, pastizzi* (see pages 36 and 40), ravioli and some desserts.

SEAFOOD
The waters of Malta are abundant with fish, including octopus, squid, shellfish and the treasured *lampuki* (mahi-mahi) that migrates north in autumn.

SHEEP'S MILK CHEESE
Small cheeselets called *ġbejniet* come fresh, semi-dried and rolled in pepper. Included on a *platt Malti* and completing many dishes.

SHORTCRUST PASTRY
Used in savoury and sweet recipes and encasing any manner of things from ricotta to fish and even pasta.

TOMATOES
Every which way! Used to create the base of stews, and particularly loved as tomato paste (concentrated purée), which is known as *kunserva*.

GRAZING

Malta's hot summer days and endless beach outings have created a culture of grazing over cold preparations.

A traditional platter of cheeses, meats and dips is known as *platt Malti*. Looked at more closely, it's really a collection of preserved foods: sausage, dried or pickled vegetables, olives, soft and hard cheeses. They are almost always served with *ħobż* (crusty white bread) or *galletti* (water crackers), both of which feature in the Breads chapter (page 65).

One hero among the mix of goodies is *ġbejniet* (sheep's milk cheese), which can be enjoyed fresh, peppered and semi-dried. Olives are also imperative to any *platt Malti*. The climate of Malta couldn't be better for growing them. Over the past 20 years, there's been a push to boost the country's olive production. Notably, resident Sam Cremona has brought to the fore the *bidni* and *perla* Maltese varieties that are unique to Malta. The latter, a white olive, became popular during the rule of the Knights of Malta, and until Sam's efforts they had almost become extinct.

Pies also frequent the Maltese diet, sweet and savoury. In most *pastizzerias*, alongside Malta's own pies, you can also find chicken and mushroom pies – a hangover from British colonisation.

This chapter also collects some of the snacks of Malta, such as the iconic *pastizzi*. Together, this is perfect entertaining food to be enjoyed outside, with cold drinks in anticipation of a meal – or why not make the *platt Malti* a meal unto itself? *Saħħa!*

ŻEBBUĠ MIMLI
STUFFED OLIVES

PREPARATION: 20 MINUTES COOKING: 30 MINUTES IF CRUMBING

I love these olives – a Maltese mega mix of flavours. You can adjust the stuffing as you like, and, for an indulgent option, crumbing and frying the olives makes them even more delicious.

INGREDIENTS

600 g (1 lb 5 oz) large pitted
  green olives
1 tablespoon extra-virgin olive oil
  (omit if crumbing)

STUFFING

180 g (6½ oz) tinned tuna in oil
3 anchovy fillets, finely chopped
2 tablespoons dry breadcrumbs
1 tablespoon capers, rinsed
  and chopped
1 garlic clove, crushed
3 tablespoons chopped flat-leaf
  (Italian) parsley
grated zest of ½ lemon
2 tablespoons extra-virgin olive oil

CRUMBING (OPTIONAL)

75 g (2¾ oz/½ cup) plain
  (all-purpose) flour
100 g (3½ oz/1 cup) dry breadcrumbs
1 egg
500 ml (17 fl oz/2 cups) neutral oil for
  frying such as sunflower or canola

HOW TO

To make the stuffing, drain the tuna. Put in a food processor with the remaining ingredients and blend to a smooth paste. If you don't have a piping bag, you can snip a 1 cm (½ in) corner from a zip-lock bag to use for stuffing the olives. Simply squeeze the mixture inside the cavity of each pitted olive. Chill the stuffed olives in the refrigerator for 1 hour. If you are going to enjoy the olives fresh, gently stir the olive oil through them and serve with toothpicks.

To crumb the olives, put the flour and breadcrumbs on separate plates. Crack the egg into a bowl and whisk. Give half the olives a light dusting in flour. Now add them to the egg wash, then use a fork to roll them one at a time in breadcrumbs and place on a plate. Repeat with the remaining olives.

Heat the oil in a heavy-based saucepan, and gently lower a crumbed olive into the oil to check if it sizzles. Fry the olives in 2 batches until the crumbs are golden brown. Drain on paper towel and serve.

QASSATAT

PREPARATION: 40 MINUTES + 45 MINUTES RESTING COOKING: 40 MINUTES

Qassatat is a word derived from the Sicilian *cassata*, which is thought to stem from the Latin *caseus*, meaning cheese – the most traditional filling of these pies. This street food is consumed second only to *pastizzi*, and wherever you find *pastizzi* in Malta, this is likely to be sitting to the side. This recipe has a spinach and anchovy filling, but to make cheese *qassatat*, use the filling on page 40 (the pea filling can also be used). Or try making them filled with ricotta and raisins as is done on the island of Gozo.

PASTRY

500 g (1 lb 2 oz) plain (all-purpose)
  flour, plus extra for dusting
1 teaspoon salt
250 g (9 oz) chilled butter, diced
2 eggs – 1 lightly beaten, for brushing
60 ml (2 fl oz/¼ cup) iced water

SPINACH AND
ANCHOVY FILLING

800 g (1 lb 12 oz) English spinach
1 tablespoon olive oil
1 medium onion, finely diced
1 garlic clove, finely chopped
4 anchovy fillets, chopped, plus
  1 teaspoon oil from the jar
50 g (1¾ oz) green olives,
  pitted and finely chopped
1 egg
1 teaspoon cornflour (cornstarch)
salt and pepper

HOW TO

Start by rubbing the flour, salt and butter together with your fingers until the mixture resembles breadcrumbs or rough sand. Mix in 1 egg, then gradually add the water to form a dough. Shape into a ball, then press into a disc and cover in plastic wrap. Chill for 45 minutes.

For the spinach and anchovy filling, slice off the spinach roots, then wash and drain the leaves. Remove the excess water by tipping onto a clean tea towel (dish towel) and patting dry. Chop smaller at the stem end, larger at the leaf end. Heat the oil in a frying pan over a low–medium heat and sauté the onion, garlic, anchovies and their oil until soft (about 8–10 minutes). Increase the heat and add the spinach and olives, cooking until the spinach wilts. Leave to cool.

Whisk the egg and cornflour together in a large bowl. Drain off any water from the spinach and stir the spinach mixture into the egg, then season with salt and pepper.

Roll the pastry out on a floured surface and cut into circles 15 cm (6 in) in diameter. Put a heaped spoon of filling in the middle of a circle and wet the edges of the pastry with a little water. Bring the pastry sides up over the filling but leave a gap where you can see the filling in the centre, and pleat the edges all around like a money bag. Continue making pies with the remaining pastry and filling.

Preheat the oven to 180°C (360°F). Brush the pastry with the lightly beaten egg. Bake the pies in the oven for 25–30 minutes, until golden.

FAŻOLA BAJDA BIT-TEWM U T-TURSIN

WHITE BEAN SALAD

PREPARATION: 10 MINUTES + OVERNIGHT SOAKING + CHILLING COOKING: 1 HOUR 15 MINUTES

This refreshing, simple salad gets a zing from a generous slosh of vinegar. It's perfect to accompany meats and seafood, but can be made more substantial, into a meal of its own, with the addition of ingredients such as tuna, diced tomato, olives and capers.

INGREDIENTS

400 g (14 oz) giant white beans
  (gigante beans) or lima beans,
  soaked overnight
2 tablespoons extra-virgin olive oil
2 spring onions (scallions),
  finely chopped
1 garlic clove, crushed
1 handful flat-leaf (Italian) parsley,
  roughly chopped
3 tablespoons red-wine
  or sherry vinegar
salt and pepper

HOW TO

Drain and rinse the soaked beans, tip into a large saucepan and cover with fresh water (at least 5 times the volume of the beans). Bring to the boil, then reduce to a simmer and cook for about 1¼ hours, until the beans are soft. Drain and rinse the cooked beans in cold water.

Put the beans in a bowl and add half the oil and all the remaining ingredients. Gently mix together and season to taste. Serve immediately or chill the salad in the refrigerator for an hour or two, allowing the beans to absorb the flavours. You can enjoy the salad cold, or bring it back to room temperature. Drizzle with the remaining oil before serving.

PASTIZZI

MAKES 12-15
PASTRIES

<u>PREPARATION</u>: 1½ HOURS + OVERNIGHT REFRIGERATION <u>COOKING</u>: 35 MINUTES

Pastizzi are enjoyed by revellers of the night, fishermen at wee hours, or office clerks bridging the gap between meals. The demand for these pastries is inexhaustible, and the phrase '*jinbiegħu bħall-pastizzi*' means 'selling like *pastizzi*', much like the English 'selling like hotcakes'. This recipe includes both the classic ricotta cheese filling and a pea filling, which is thought to have crept in during England's sovereignty of Malta. It is best to make the dough and fillings a day in advance. I should note that *pastizzi* are difficult to make, which is why I have included a 'cheat's method' at the end of this recipe. Working on a smooth stone surface or the like is recommended. The main objective is to make a roll of dough with as many buttered layers as possible. The pastry has a mixture of lard and margarine, making it more stable and easier to work with compared to pastry made with butter. Once you are performing the feats of rolling and stretching, you will see why.

PASTRY

220 g (8 oz) margarine at
 room temperature
 (plus extra for brushing)
60 g (2 oz) lard at
 room temperature
450 g (1 lb/3 cups) plain
 (all-purpose) flour
1½ teaspoons salt
220 ml (7 fl oz) water
 plus 1 tablespoon if needed
olive oil for shaping

RICOTTA FILLING

150 ml (5 fl oz) water
20 g (¾ oz) butter
50 g (1¾ oz) fine semolina
1 small egg
½ teaspoon salt
¼ teaspoon freshly ground
 black pepper
500 g (1 lb 2 oz) ricotta

PEA FILLING

1 medium onion, finely diced
2 garlic cloves, finely chopped
1 tablespoon olive oil
½ teaspoon ground allspice
1 tablespoon tomato paste
 (concentrated purée)
400 g (14 oz) peas, blanched if fresh
 or rinsed if frozen
salt and pepper

HOW TO

To make the pastry, mix the margarine and lard together and set aside. Combine the flour, salt and water in a bowl and mix until you have a dry but well-combined dough. Transfer to a work surface and knead until smooth. Take a rolling pin and bash the dough into a rectangular shape running lengthways away from you. Now roll it back and forth until 4 cm (1.5 in) thick. Roll the rectangle up into a log, then spin it 90 degrees so the log is running lengthways again. Repeat the process of bashing down, rolling out, rolling up and spinning 8–10 times. This creates a dough that is elastic and firm. Finally form the dough into a ball, and use your hands to lather a quarter of the margarine mixture all over it. Place in a large plastic bag and refrigerate for 1 hour.

Take the dough out of the refrigerator – it should no longer be springy to touch. Use your hands to press the dough into a rectangle, this time running crossways on the bench. Rest a hand in the centre of the dough while you use your other hand to pull and stretch the dough longer on one side. Swap hands and stretch the other side. Stretch until the dough is about 50 cm (20 in) long and 15 cm (6 in) wide. Now roll the dough out a little bigger, until ½–1 cm (¼–½ in) thick, around 70 cm (27½ in) long and 20 cm (8 in) wide. Lather the surface of the dough with another half of the margarine mixture (reserving a quarter).

Use the palm of your hand to stick one end of the dough to the bench. At the opposite end, start rolling the dough into a log while at the same time, gently pulling back and stretching the dough thinner. Be careful not to tear the dough, and also try to roll tightly to avoid air pockets. Once you reach the end, the log may be thinner at the ends and fatter in the middle; if so, tuck or push in the ends so the log has a similar diameter throughout. Lather the remaining margarine over the log. Return to the bag and refrigerate overnight.

You can also make the fillings a day in advance (and it's easier to make *pastizzi* using chilled filling). For the ricotta filling, in a saucepan bring the water and butter to the boil and whisk in the semolina, then turn off the heat. In a mixing bowl, whisk the egg with the salt and pepper, then add the ricotta and whisk to combine. Mix in the semolina and transfer to the refrigerator.

For the pea filling, sauté the onion and garlic with the oil and allspice in a frying pan. Add the tomato paste and peas. Add splashes of water to help the peas cook; you want them to crack and you may need to use a fork to mash them slightly. Season with salt and pepper and mash the peas in the pan. Transfer to a bowl and chill in the refrigerator.

The next day, line some baking trays with baking paper, and place your fillings on the bench. Pour some olive oil into a small bowl. Take the pastry log from the bag and gently stretch it until it doubles in length, and about 5 cm (2 in)

wide. Cut the log at 5 cm (2 in) intervals to make wheels. Lay them flat so the spiral of layers face upwards. Dip your thumbs in the oil and pick up a wheel of dough, holding it in both hands with your thumbs in the centre. Pinch and spin the wheel to create a tea cup. Turn the cup inside out, stretching it a little more until the opening has a diameter of about 10 cm (4 in). Fill it with some ricotta mixture. Press the top of the pastry cup together, creating a seam. Place on a tray with the seam up, like a Cornish pastie. With your index fingers, press down on the seam 1 cm (½ in) from each edge, forming mounded pastie shapes.

To make *pastizzi* with pea filling, shape and fill them in the same way, but place them on the tray with the seams on the side.

Bake the *pastizzi* in a preheated 220°C (430°F) oven for 25 minutes, until golden brown.

This requires a pasta machine. After the first refrigeration of the dough, split the dough into two pieces. Use a rolling pin to flatten out one piece to a rectangle about the width of your hand. Start feeding the piece through the machine on its widest setting. Decrease the width by a notch and roll the sheet through again. Continue until the sheet is around 90 cm (3 ft) long. Now lay the sheet on your work surface and use the rolling pin to roll the sheet wider. You should be able to get it to 15–20 cm (6–8 in) across its length. Lather the surface of the sheet with another quarter of the margarine mixture. Stick an end to the bench and roll up and stretch as above. Repeat with the second piece of dough. Lather both logs in the remaining margarine, return to the bag and refrigerate overnight. The next day, stretch the logs until about 5 cm (2 in) wide and cut and make pastizzi *as above.*

BIGILLA

TIC BEAN DIP

PREPARATION: 10 MINUTES + OVERNIGHT SOAKING   COOKING: 1 HOUR 45 MINUTES

This dip closely resembles Egyptian *ful*. The Sacco family operate a *bigilla* van touring towns of Malta most afternoons, selling the paste warm from the back of the vehicle. If the van is close you will hear it, with the driver yelling '*bigilla*' over a megaphone. Tradition suggests the dip is served warm with chopped parsley and chilli oil at your discretion (or you can use olive oil if you don't want the spice). *Galletti* (page 74) or warm bread is mandatory on the side. *Bigilla* also happens to be delicious cold, keeps well, and can even be used to stuff artichokes. Tic beans are known in Malta as *djerba* – they are a smaller, darker bean than broad (fava) beans, and are sometimes called field or horse beans. Short of finding tic beans, you can use whole dried broad (fava) beans.

INGREDIENTS

250 g (9 oz) dried tic beans
  (or dried broad/fava beans),
  soaked overnight
2 tablespoons olive oil
1 teaspoon salt
1 garlic clove, crushed
½ teaspoon chilli flakes
2 tablespoons chopped
  flat-leaf (Italian) parsley

TO GARNISH

2 teaspoons chilli flakes
80 ml (2½ fl oz/⅓ cup) olive oil
1 tablespoon chopped
  flat-leaf (Italian) parsley

HOW TO

Drain and rinse the soaked beans and tip into a large saucepan. Cover with fresh water (at least 5 times the volume of the beans) and bring to the boil. Reduce to a simmer and scoop any foam from the surface. Loosely cover the pan with a lid and let the beans simmer for about 1¾ hours until soft, topping up the water if needed.

Meanwhile, prepare the chilli oil for the garnish by toasting the chilli flakes in a pan and adding the oil when the chilli is fragrant. Remove from the heat and pour into a small bowl or jar to infuse.

When the beans are soft, scoop out a cup of the cooking water and drain the beans. Put the beans in a food processor, together with 3 tablespoons of cooking water and the remaining ingredients. Pulse until you have a paste. Add more water if the dip seems too thick.

To serve, scoop the dip into a bowl and garnish with the chilli oil and parsley.

ĠBEJNIET

SHEEP'S MILK CHEESELETS

PREPARATION: 2 HOURS 30 MINUTES + OVERNIGHT REFRIGERATION COOKING: 5 MINUTES

Ġbejniet can be likened to ricotta, but made from sheep's milk and with a texture that is far superior. Think of crème caramel or silken tofu in its early stages of setting. Sheep are much more suited to Malta's rocky landscape than cows, so it makes sense that *ġbejniet* was always made with their milk. If we were to go back in time, it's likely any Maltese recipe mentioning 'ricotta' was made with sheep's or goat's milk. The British brought with them cattle and incentives to discontinue production of sheep's milk, so today many versions of *ġbejniet* are made with cow's milk. But you can make *ġbejniet* at home! (And of course, this recipe also works for cow's milk.) Fresh *ġbejniet* keeps for a few days, but is best eaten as soon as possible. And the fresher the milk is, the better the cheese tastes. *Ġbejniet* can also be dried and preserved (see overpage) to give them a longer shelf life. Drying them gives the cheese a texture similar to that of a harder cheese such as pecorino.

Semi-dried *ġbejniet* is excellent grated onto pastas and other dishes as you would parmesan. It can also be broken up and used in stews or salads, or added to the cheese filling for *pastizzi*.

INGREDIENTS

2 litres (68 fl oz/8 cups)
  unhomogenised sheep's milk
  (the higher the fat content the
  better; use homogenised milk in
  countries such as New Zealand
  where brucellosis can be present)
1½ teaspoons rennet powder
sea salt

EQUIPMENT

6–8 *ġbejniet* cheese baskets
  (*qwieleb*), about 8 cm (3¼ in)
  wide and 6 cm (2½ in) high
  (alternatively, you could use
  1 larger ricotta basket)
kitchen thermometer

HOW TO

Heat the milk gently in a heavy-based saucepan. Once it reaches 38°C (100°F) on a thermometer, turn off the heat. Take 3 table-spoons of the warm milk in a small glass and stir in the rennet. Now stir this back into the pan of milk. Leave for 1 hour.

Use a sharp knife to make some cuts through the semi-set milk. Leave for another 30 minutes.

Use a slotted spoon (or one of your cheese baskets) to scoop the curd and start filling the baskets. Top them up as the whey starts draining out, ensuring they are filled as high as possible. When you have scooped all the curd, sprinkle salt generously over the top of each cheese. Place the baskets on a wire rack set above a tray and allow to drain for 1 hour.

Turn the cheeses upside down in their baskets and sprinkle again with salt. Transfer the cheese, rack and tray to the refrigerator and allow to drain for another 8 hours or overnight. After this, the cheese can be turned out and is ready to eat. (The cheese can also be enjoyed after just a few hours of draining – the jelly-like texture is marvellous.)

ĠBEJNIET MOXXI

Follow the recipe on page 46 to make the cheese. Leave your cheeselets out on a wire rack for 1 day in an area that is well ventilated and cool, without humidity. A draught or a fan can help create the ideal conditions. The next day, sprinkle the top of the cheeses with more salt, and turn over and dry for at least 2 more days, or until the cheeses have visibly shrunk, are light yellow in colour, and are firm and waxy to the centre with a crumbly texture (cut a cheese to check). The exact length of drying time depends on the conditions. Keep the finished cheeses in a sealed container in the refrigerator, where they should keep for a few weeks or so.

ĠBEJNIET TAL-BŻAR

Peppered cheeselets (*ġbejniet tal-bżar*): dry the cheeselets for 2 days. Fill a small plate with white-wine vinegar, and another with freshly ground black pepper. Roll the cheeselets in vinegar, and then pepper until evenly coated. Continue drying the cheese (see page 46).

To preserve semi-dried *ġbejniet*: Combine 1 part water and 2 parts white-wine vinegar in a clean jar. Add the semi-dried cheeselets (plain or peppered) and ensure they are submerged. Store in the refrigerator for at least 1 week. Drain off four-fifths of the vinegar, and add one-fifth olive oil (the cheeselets will no longer be submerged). Gently roll the cheeselets around in the jar to coat in the oil and vinegar. Return to the refrigerator, and occasionally turn the jar upside down. The cheeselets will keep for months.

SFINEĠ TAL-INĊOVA

ANCHOVY FRITTERS

PREPARATION: 25 MINUTES + 1 HOUR PROVING COOKING: 10 MINUTES

At Easter time in the city of Rabat, you can find stalls selling these on every corner. They are similar to the Saint Joseph's fritters with ricotta (page 214), but savoury with an anchovy inside. They are more-ish served alongside a cold beer or dry white wine.

INGREDIENTS

225 g (8 oz/1½ cups) plain
  (all-purpose) flour
2 teaspoons dried yeast
½ teaspoon salt
180 ml (6 fl oz) warm water
1 litre (34 fl oz/4 cups) neutral oil
  for frying such as sunflower or
  canola, plus extra for oiling
10 anchovy fillets
lemon wedges, to serve

HOW TO

In a large bowl, combine the flour, yeast and salt with a wooden spoon and make a well in the centre. Gradually add the water to the well, gently mixing until all the flour has been incorporated and you have a sticky dough. Tip onto a floured work bench and knead for a few minutes until you have a smooth dough. Shape into a ball and lightly oil the dough. Return to the bowl. Cover with a tea towel (dish towel) and set aside in a warm place to prove for 1 hour, or until the dough has doubled in size.

Begin to gently heat the oil in a heavy-based saucepan. Lightly flour your hands and divide the dough into 10 pieces. Take a lump of dough and gently stretch it to an oval shape. Lay an anchovy in the centre and close the dough around it. Lower the fritter into the hot oil while you quickly make a few more fritters to cook at the same time. Flip the fritters over once and cook until golden brown (around 2½ minutes). Scoop onto paper towel. Check the fritters are cooked through by eating the first one! Continue to make and cook the remaining fritters. Serve with lemon wedges.

BARBULJATA

MALTESE SCRAMBLED EGGS

PREPARATION: 10 MINUTES   COOKING: 10 MINUTES

I have strong memories of my uncle making this for breakfast. He would emphasise how the mint makes all the difference. The recipe was passed down from his aunt, and forever holds a place in my all-day-breakfast repertoire. The sweet onion combined with the acidity of the tomatoes and the refreshing mint lift scrambled eggs out of the mundane and into glorious territory. I love a touch of cumin, but this is optional. Needless to say, freshly baked ħobż on the side is a must, or you could serve it on toasted sourdough.

INGREDIENTS

2 large ripe tomatoes
1 red onion, finely chopped
1 tablespoon olive oil
¼ teaspoon ground cumin (optional)
6 eggs
½ teaspoon salt
1 tablespoon chopped mint
freshly ground black pepper

HOW TO

Bring a small saucepan of water to the boil. Score the tomatoes on their bases and add them to the boiling water for 1½–2 minutes. Remove with tongs to a bowl of iced water. When the tomatoes are cool enough to handle, peel them, scoop out the seeds and discard, and dice the flesh into 1 cm (½ in) pieces.

Sauté the onion with the oil and cumin (if using) in a frying pan over a low–medium heat. Cook until the onion is soft. Meanwhile, crack the eggs into a bowl and whisk with the salt. Increase the heat of the pan and stir the tomato into the onion, cooking for a couple of minutes. Then add the eggs, mint and some pepper. Scramble the eggs with the tomato until just cooked. Check the seasoning and serve.

Pull the handbrake; breathe out after the steepest, narrowest road.
Heat overwhelms you descending the rocky path, but not for long.
Set camp, towels, *ftira* and cold drinks.
The flickering water, that lapping sound.
It's just there, no need to rush.
Wade up to your neck, level your temperature; it's perfect.
Swim out, take a deep breath, tuck the knees, descend.
Body roll, look up, breathe out, you're there.
A swim into the deep blue.

ARJOLI
TUNA TOMATO DIP

PREPARATION: 10 MINUTES

This dip is one of those recipes that gets tweaked and leveraged in many ways. *Arjoli* is a melting pot of classic Maltese flavours, but you can use what's on hand in the fridge or pantry, omitting and adding to it ingredients such as capers, preserved artichokes, mint, beans, sun-dried tomatoes and spring onion (scallion). The dip is perfect spread over crusty ħobż or with *Galletti* (page 74). You can even keep it cold and pack it for the beach.

INGREDIENTS

180 g (6½ oz) tinned tuna in oil,
  drained
3 anchovy fillets, chopped
200 g (7 oz) tomato paste
  (concentrated purée)
1 small onion, chopped
1 garlic clove, finely chopped
50 g (1¾ oz) kalamata olives, pitted
100 g (4½ oz) *Galletti* (page 74)
  or water crackers
3 tablespoons chopped
  flat-leaf (Italian) parsley
1 pinch of chilli flakes
180 ml (6 fl oz) extra-virgin olive oil
2 teaspoons red-wine vinegar,
  plus extra to taste

HOW TO

First blitz the crackers in the food processor until they have broken down. Now add all ingredients and blitz to a paste. If it seems dry, add a splash of water. Taste the dip and add more vinegar if desired. Serve with slices of crusty bread or *galletti*.

BAKED EGGPLANT AND ONION WITH BASIL

PREPARATION: 10 MINUTES COOKING: 50 MINUTES

Over a selection of Maltese snacks, Gozitan restaurateur Phillip Spiteri described this dish to me. It is such an easy recipe – actually two individual spreads to be served side by side. The eggplant and onion are perfect with roasted meats and fish, or included on a *platt Malti*. I'm sure once you've made this, it will become a staple in your kitchen as it has in mine. The recipe fortifies the Maltese cooking mantra: quality ingredients and simple technique equate to greatness.

INGREDIENTS

2 onions
1 large eggplant (aubergine)
3 tablespoons extra-virgin olive oil
2 handfuls basil leaves
salt

HOW TO

Preheat the oven to 220°C (430°F). Take a short, sharp-tipped knife and stab through the skin of the onions, making 6 small incisions around each one. Roast on a baking tray for 20 minutes. Now make 6 incisions around the eggplant and add to the onions, roasting for another 30 minutes.

Allow the vegetables to cool until you are able to handle them, then make a cut lengthways through the skins. Squeeze out the onion flesh into a wide bowl, and the eggplant flesh into another.

Divide the oil and basil between the bowls. Season with salt and use the back of a fork to mash the soft flesh with the oil and basil. Scoop the eggplant onto a plate and the onion alongside. This is best served at room temperature, but can also be warmed again if desired.

BREADS

The feather in the cap of Maltese bread is its crust. Nowhere else in the world have I bitten into a darkish-coloured loaf with a crust that manages to be so light.

No day passes in Malta without *ftira* being slathered in *kunserva* (Maltese tomato paste) or sliced *ħobż* being served alongside a meal. Bread plays a huge role in the archipelago's cuisine. The word for bread is in many Maltese idioms, one of which is '*Xhobx jiekol dak*', which means 'What bread does he eat?' It is used when asking about the good or bad character of someone.

In 1919, post-war Malta was in a desperate and needy state. A series of hikes in the cost of flour conspired with a growing dissatisfaction in colonial rule, sparking an uprising that became known as the 'Bread Riots'. Sadly, four men perished in the ruckus at the hands of English soldiers. They are honoured annually on *Sette Giugno* (7th June), marking this moment where the Maltese fought for what they believed in and their voices were heard.

Throughout Malta, every city or town has a local bakery, often housing a wood-fired stone oven that churns out crusty bread from the wee hours. At these times one can easily find the baker by following one's nose. As a customer you don't enter the bakery; rather you make your selection as you peer inside the door from the street. With the aromas knocking you off your feet, it's hard not to buy everything on offer.

Maltese bread is not some perfect alchemy of different grains and fermentation. You could say *ħobż* is a basic white loaf, while *ftira* is made from the same dough but has a hole in the middle. The feather in its cap is the crust. Nowhere else in the world have I bitten into a darkish-coloured loaf with crust that manages to be light to the crunch. It sends a raucous sound up to your ears, and then there is enormous contrast as you reach the fluffy interior. Just delicious.

As white breads, *ħobż* and *ftira* don't share the longevity of some of the world's other breads. But they are perfect for being turned into breadcrumbs. Leftover bread and breadcrumbs get used in many Maltese dishes including stuffings and desserts.

ĦOBŻ U FTIRA
MALTESE BREAD

PREPARATION: 30 MINUTES + 10-12 HOURS PROVING COOKING: 40 MINUTES

Ħobż is the Maltese word for bread. Essentially a white loaf, oval to round in shape, which takes on a serious crust on the top and sides (except for the sides that crowd up next to other loaves while being baked – although this won't happen at home unless you're cooking for the masses). *Ftira* is the same bread that takes a flatter form: ring-shaped, like a huge bagel. Custom implores you to slice open a *ftira* and fill it with any typical Maltese toppings (see the suggestions below), then carve it into portions. Both *ftira* and *ħobż* can be made with the same dough, taking different shapes just before baking. This is a no-knead recipe without the usual knocking back, and a gentle hand is required. I find it best to use a cast-iron pot for *ħobż* to keep its form high and help those critical crusty edges materialise.

CHEAT'S STARTER

125 g (4½ oz) plain (all-purpose) flour
1½ teaspoons dried yeast
120 ml (4 fl oz) warm water

260 g (9 oz) strong white flour,
  plus extra for dusting
2 teaspoons dried yeast
1 teaspoon salt
180 ml (6 fl oz) warm water
45 ml (1½ fl oz) milk

FTIRA FILLINGS

Here are some typical combinations to sandwich in *ftira*, although you can mix and match at will.

• Squashed ripe tomato, *ġbejniet*, capers, mint and extra-virgin olive oil

• Anchovies, *kunserva* (tomato paste), extra-virgin olive oil and capers

• *Kunserva*, red onion, tinned tuna, *giardiniera* (pickled vegetables), olives, capers and shredded lettuce

HOW TO

Make the starter 8 hours ahead (you could mix it just before going to bed to prove overnight). Combine the ingredients in a large bowl and stir. Cover with plastic wrap and leave at room temperature for 8 hours. If in a very warm environment, place in the fridge for 10 hours.

Add the remaining ingredients to the starter and stir with a fork to begin with. Swap to a wooden spoon and form the dough into a ball. Cover with a tea towel (dish towel) and leave in a warm place for 30 minutes.

Add a good sprinkle of flour around the edges of the dough and use a spoon or flexible spatula to loosen the dough from the bowl. Use your hands to gently fold the dough in on itself 10 times in the bowl. The dough will feel sticky at first, but will become easier to handle as some of the flour is incorporated. Leave to rest for another 30 minutes.

Sprinkle more flour around the edges and ease the dough from the sides of the bowl. Repeat the 10 folds and allow to rest another 30 minutes.

Dust a good amount of flour over baking paper. Let the dough gently drop onto the paper and gently form a dome shape by carefully cupping your hands and tucking under the edges. You don't want to knock air out of the dough. If making *ħobż*, cover the dough with a tea towel. If making *ftira*, form a hole in the middle of the dough using the base of a glass. Leave the glass in the hole, then drape the tea towel (dish towel) over the glass. For both styles of loaf, leave for 25 minutes, until it begins to rise.

Preheat the oven to 250°C (480°F). Heat a cast-iron pot in the oven if making *ħobż*, or a pizza stone or baking tray if making *ftira*. Slide the loaf with paper on the stone (*ftira*) or into the hot pot (*ħobż*). Be as careful as possible not to knock the air from the dough. For *ftira*, work the hole back into the middle of the loaf, exaggerating the size of the hole as it will close up in the oven. Spray your loaf with a mist or sprinkles of water, which will help it to develop a crust. Bake in the hot oven for 35 minutes (*ftira*) or 40 minutes (*ħobż*), until dark brown on the outside and sounding hollow when tapped. Let the loaf cool completely on a wire rack.

GALLETTI
WATER CRACKERS

MAKES ABOUT
45 CRACKERS

<u>PREPARATION</u>: 25 MINUTES + 1 HOUR 10 MINUTES PROVING + 1-2 HOURS DRYING
<u>COOKING</u>: 6 MINUTES

This water biscuit is an icon of Maltese cuisine, traditionally loved by fishermen as it travelled well at sea. Today it's essential to accompany any *platt Malti*. *Galletti* are also common as a snack, even sold in Maltese sausage flavour!

<u>INGREDIENTS</u>

170 ml (5½ fl oz/⅔ cup) warm water
1 teaspoon dried yeast
1 tablespoon olive oil
200 g (7 oz/1⅓ cups) plain
 (all-purpose) flour
150 g (5½ oz) fine semolina
½ teaspoon salt

<u>HOW TO</u>

Mix the water, yeast and oil together in a mixing bowl and leave for 10 minutes. Stir in the flour, semolina and salt. Knead on a lightly floured surface for 10 minutes, until you have a smooth, elastic dough. Return the dough to the bowl, cover with a tea towel (dish towel) and leave in a warm place for 1 hour, until beginning to rise. (Alternatively, you can make the dough in a stand mixer fitted with a dough hook.)

Knock the air out of the dough and transfer to your work surface. Cut into 3 portions and let the pieces rest for 10 minutes.

Preheat the oven to 230°C (445°F). Working with one piece at a time,

roll out to a large shape 2 mm (⅛ in) thick. Use a round cutter (about 6 cm/2½ in) or an upturned glass to cut crackers. Place at least 3 cm (1¼ in) apart on baking trays lined with baking paper. Prick each cracker twice with a fork. Continue to roll out, cut and prick *galletti* with the remaining pieces of dough, and then with the dough scraps. Bake the *galletti* for 3 minutes, then flip them all and bake for 3 minutes longer. Remove the trays from the oven and leave the door open for a few minutes to expel some heat. Return the trays to the oven and allow the *galletti* to cool down and dry out for 1–2 hours. Store in a sealed container.

FTIRA GĦAWDXIJA

PIZZA BREAD FROM GOZO

MAKES
1 BREAD

<u>PREPARATION</u>: 15 MINUTES + 2 HOURS PROVING <u>COOKING</u>: 20 MINUTES

The age-old recipe for this 'pizza' actually used a sourdough flatbread (hence '*ftira*' in the name) to envelop its fillings. The bread can be traced back to the village of Nadur on Gozo, where two bakeries still make versions of the original today. It can have any of the likely Maltese fillings: olives, capers, tomato … But what distinguishes Gozitan *ftira* is how the filling bakes inside like a calzone, only with an open top. Let's call it a savoury free-form pie!

The most traditional and delicious filling is *ġbejniet* cheese with thinly sliced potato on top. If you don't have the cheese handy, you can substitute ricotta. Likewise, peppered pecorino (or parmesan plus pepper) can be used instead of the semi-dried peppered *ġbejniet*.

<u>INGREDIENTS</u>

175 ml (6 fl oz) warm water
1 teaspoon dried yeast
1 tablespoon olive oil
250 g (9 oz/1⅔ cups)
  strong white flour
½ teaspoon salt
1–2 tablespoons fine semolina,
  for rolling

<u>FILLING</u>

3 medium eggs
1 teaspoon salt
4–5 fresh *Ġbejniet* cheeselets
  (page 46) or 400 g (14 oz)
  firm ricotta
2 semi-dried peppered *ġbejniet*
  cheeselets (pages 46–47) or 80 g
  (2¾ oz) peppered pecorino, grated
1 large potato, peeled and thinly
  sliced (use a mandoline if you
  have one)
1 tablespoon olive oil

<u>HOW TO</u>

Combine the water, yeast and oil in a mixing bowl and set aside for a few minutes. Add the flour and salt and form into a dough. Knead for 10 minutes until smooth and elastic. (Alternatively, make the dough in a stand mixer fitted with a dough hook.) Return to the bowl, cover with a tea towel (dish towel) and leave for 1½ hours.

Knock the air out of the dough, remove it from the bowl and dust it in the semolina. Roll into a thick disc, then cover and leave for another 30 minutes.

Meanwhile, prepare the filling. First whisk the eggs with the salt before mixing in the cheeses. In a separate bowl, toss the potato with the oil and some extra salt, making sure the slices are evenly coated.

Preheat the oven to 220°C (430°F). If you have a pizza stone, place it in the oven (otherwise heat a baking tray). Roll the dough out to a 40 cm (15¾ in) circle. Spread the cheese mixture in the centre, leaving a 10 cm (4 in) border. Distribute the potato slices evenly over the top of the cheese. Fold in the sides of the dough, gently stretching them upwards before placing them down. The *ftira* should remain open in the middle. Bake in the oven for 15–20 minutes, until the bread and potatoes are golden brown. Cut into wedges and serve with a salad.

QAGHAQ TAL-HMIRA
YEAST RINGS

PREPARATION: 20 MINUTES + 2 HOURS 40 MINUTES PROVING COOKING: 15 MINUTES

These spiced buns sit between sweet and savoury, and are reminiscent of hot cross buns only without the fruit. Served with butter and/or jam, freshly baked yeast rings are perfect for afternoon tea.

INGREDIENTS

165 ml (5½ fl oz) milk

80 g (2¾ oz) sugar

2 teaspoons dried yeast

350 g (12½ oz/2⅓ cups)
  strong white flour,
  plus extra for dusting

¼ teaspoon salt

1 teaspoon mixed
  (pumpkin pie) spice

grated zest of 1 small orange

grated zest of 1 small lemon

70 g (2½ oz) butter

50 g (1¾ oz/⅓ cup) sesame seeds

HOW TO

Heat the milk with 2 teaspoons of the sugar until warm to touch. Pour into a mixing bowl and add the yeast. Set aside for 10 minutes.

Add the flour, salt, spice, citrus zest, butter and remaining sugar to the bowl. Mix into a dough, then knead for 10 minutes until smooth and elastic. (Alternatively, make the dough in a stand mixer fitted with a dough hook.) Cover with a tea towel (dish towel) and leave to rise for 2 hours.

On a lightly floured surface, divide the dough into 8 even pieces. Roll into strips 20–25 cm (8–10 in)

long. They should be about 3 cm (1¼ in) thick. Take a strip and lightly wet one end. Loop the dough into a ring with the ends slightly overlapping and press them together. Place the rings on baking trays lined with baking paper, allowing a few centimetres (1 inch) of space between them. Brush lightly with a little extra milk or water and generously sprinkle with the sesame seeds. Cover and leave to rise for 30 minutes.

Preheat the oven to 180°C (360°F). Bake the rings in the oven for 15 minutes.

PASTA

Spaghetti with tomato sauce is a mainstay of the Maltese diet, and larger or celebratory meals typically start with pasta.

Malta's proximity to Sicily and Italy has given pasta a firm foothold in the cuisine. Spaghetti and macaroni (straight rather than elbow shaped) are commonly used, as well as *kusksu*, a small bead-shaped pasta that resembles Sardinian *fregola*, and whose name seems to echo 'couscous'.

Spaghetti with tomato sauce is a mainstay of the Maltese diet, and larger or celebratory meals typically start with pasta. For example, when a family is eating rabbit or octopus stew, the sauce is often served with pasta as an entree or as leftovers the day after.

Absent fanciful shapes and complex sauces, Maltese cuisine uses pasta to embrace a relatively small selection of ingredients. Yet simple pairings of meat, fresh cheese, tomato and seafood are prepared in inventive fashion. From a vermicelli omelette to small pasta cooked like risotto, this chapter offers an array of comforting recipes worth repeating.

SPAGETTI RIZZI

SEA URCHIN SPAGHETTI

SERVES 4

<u>PREPARATION</u>: 10 MINUTES <u>COOKING</u>: 15 MINUTES

When writing about this dish, in my mind I'm exploring craggy rocks beside the Mediterranean, dodging urchins under foot while Malta's sun beams down on me. This dish takes you to the seaside. The flavour of the sea penetrates through the pasta – a dish so simple that for me it typifies Maltese food, especially when served with crusty bread and a green salad. Purists might leave the lemon and mint out of the dish, but I love their freshness (if you prefer, you can substitute parsley for mint). The orange flesh inside sea urchins is actually a reproductive organ, sometimes deceivingly called roe. Its flavour is at its sweet and salty best before the urchins are preparing to spawn (different species do this at different times, but for many the best season to eat them is autumn). You can buy sea urchin removed from its spiny shells at good fishmongers.

<u>INGREDIENTS</u>

2 medium-sized ripe tomatoes

400 g (14 oz) spaghetti

salt and pepper

1 small onion, finely diced

1 garlic clove, finely chopped

3 tablespoons olive oil

grated zest of ¼ lemon

1 teaspoon lemon juice

1 teaspoon chopped mint

150 g (5½ oz) sea urchin flesh

<u>HOW TO</u>

Score the tomatoes on their bases and grate with a box grater. Boil the spaghetti in well-salted water until al dente. Scoop out 200 ml (7 fl oz) of the cooking water before draining the pasta.

While the pasta is cooking, sauté the onion and garlic in 2 tablespoons of the oil in a frying pan over a low–medium heat.

When the onion is soft, add the tomato and some salt and pepper and cook for 2 minutes until the tomato breaks down. Now add the pasta, its water, lemon zest and juice, mint, the remaining oil and the sea urchin. Toss together until the urchin breaks apart and distributes through the pasta. Taste for seasoning and serve.

RAVJUL ĠBEJNIET

GOZITAN RAVIOLI

PREPARATION: 40 MINUTES COOKING: 20 MINUTES

A must for travellers on Gozo is tasting restaurateur Rikardu Zammit's ravioli on the roof at restaurant Ta' Rikardu at the citadel in the centre of Victoria. He makes his own *ġbejniet* cheese and pasta, topping them with a sweet tomato sauce. The simple dish highlights the flavour of ripe tomatoes and the milky cheese – divine. For those who can't visit, this recipe aims to get you as close to the experience as possible.

PASTA

See page 102

FILLING

1 small egg
4 fresh Ġbejniet cheeselets
   (see page 46) or 360 g
   (12½ oz) firm ricotta
½ teaspoon salt
¼ teaspoon pepper

TOMATO SAUCE

3 large ripe tomatoes
½ onion, finely diced
2 garlic cloves, finely chopped
1 tablespoon olive oil
2 tablespoons tomato paste
   (concentrated purée)
2 teaspoons sugar
1 teaspoon dried oregano
salt and pepper

1 egg, lightly beaten
semolina, for dusting
chopped flat-leaf
   (Italian) parsley, to serve
extra-virgin olive oil, to serve

HOW TO

Make the pasta dough following the recipe on page 102. While it is resting, make the filling and sauce. To make the filling, whisk the egg in a mixing bowl, then mix in the cheese, salt and pepper.

To make the sauce, score the tomatoes on their bases and grate with a box grater. Sauté the onion and garlic with the oil in a saucepan over a medium heat for 5 minutes. Add the tomatoes, tomato paste, sugar, oregano and season with salt and pepper and simmer for another 8 minutes. Taste for seasoning and remove from the heat.

Cut off a third of the pasta dough and keep the rest covered. Dust the dough lightly in flour, then use a rolling pin to flatten it to a rectangle about the width of your hand. Now begin to run it through a pasta machine, starting on the widest setting. Run the piece through a few times, folding in the ragged edges between each roll, until you have a smooth sheet with straight sides. Decrease the width by a notch and roll the sheet through again. Continue decreasing the width and rolling until the sheet is around 90 cm

(3 ft) long. (You won't need to go to the narrowest setting, keeping the pasta thicker.) Set the sheet aside and roll out the other two pieces of dough.

Dollop heaped teaspoons of filling 9 cm (3½ in) apart across the pasta sheets. Use a 9 cm (3½ in) round cutter to cut out circles with the filling at the centre. Brush some of the beaten egg around the edge of the filling. Fold the pasta circles into half-moons, gently pressing the edges together. Dust a baking tray with semolina and place the ravioli on the tray. (Your pasta scraps can be cut, tossed with semolina and cooked as fresh pasta, or stored in the freezer.)

Bring 4 litres (135 fl oz/16 cups) of well-salted water to the boil. Reduce the heat to a gentle simmer and add half the ravioli. Meanwhile, gently reheat the tomato sauce. Simmer the ravioli for 3½ minutes, then scoop out with a slotted spoon onto plates. Continue cooking the remaining ravioli. Serve the ravioli with a spoonful of sauce, a sprinkle of parsley and a drizzle of extra-virgin olive oil.

BAKED PASTA SHELLS WITH RICOTTA

PREPARATION: 45 MINUTES COOKING: 1 HOUR

There are different ways of making this dish, with some people baking the pasta in the oven from raw, and others replacing the tomato sauce with béchamel. In this version, you stuff the pasta shells with ricotta before boiling them, sealing the exposed edges with semolina. The tomato is the perfect contrast to the creamy ricotta, and the shells develop crusty edges in the oven. Kids love this dish! Serve with salad and crusty bread.

INGREDIENTS

3 large ripe tomatoes or 400 g (14 oz) tinned diced tomatoes

1 onion, finely diced

1 garlic clove, finely chopped

1 tablespoon olive oil, plus extra for drizzling

2 tablespoons tomato paste (concentrated purée)

1 bay leaf

250 ml (8½ fl oz/1 cup) water

salt and pepper

400 g (14 oz) ricotta

2 eggs

1 tablespoon chopped mint

100 g (3½ oz) parmesan, finely grated

60 g (2 oz/⅓ cup) fine semolina

400 g (14 oz) large pasta shells (*lumaconi* is best, but *conchiglie* can also be used)

HOW TO

If using fresh tomatoes, score them on their bases and grate with a box grater. Sauté the onion and garlic with the oil in a saucepan over a medium heat until soft. Add the tomato paste, tomatoes, bay leaf and water. Season with salt and pepper and simmer with a lid on for 25 minutes.

Combine the ricotta, eggs, mint, a third of the parmesan, 2 tablespoons of the semolina and some salt and pepper in a bowl. Whisk the mixture together. Scoop into a piping bag, or a zip-lock bag with a 1 cm (½ in) corner snipped off. Spill the remaining semolina onto a plate. Take a pasta shell and squeeze some ricotta inside. Dip the exposed ricotta in the semolina to cover. Continue to fill and dip the pasta shells.

Bring 4 litres (135 fl oz/16 cups) of well-salted water to the boil.

Reduce the heat to a simmer and carefully add the filled shells. Simmer gently until the pasta is al dente. (Due to the filling and cooking slower than usual, the time will be different to what is stated on the packet. You will need to remove a shell from the water and break off a corner to check.) When cooked, lift shells delicately with a slotted spoon and place on a baking tray.

Preheat the oven to 190°C (375°F). Spread half the tomato sauce over the base of a large baking dish. Sprinkle another third of the parmesan on top. Place the boiled shells over the tomato and parmesan. Spread the remaining sauce over the shells, sprinkle with the remaining parmesan, and drizzle with some olive oil. Bake on the top rack of the oven for 20 minutes, just until the top is crusty and the cheese golden.

FROĠA TAT-TARJA

VERMICELLI AND PARMESAN PIE

PREPARATION: 15 MINUTES COOKING: 15 MINUTES

This curious pie, made without dough and cooked on the stovetop, is thought to have been developed by home cooks with leftover pasta. Here is the classic version, but other ingredients such as roasted vegetables or flavour bombs like capers, sun-dried tomatoes and olives can be added to the mix – you may just need to include a bit more cheese and egg to bind. The pie on its own can be dry, so I have included a sharp tomato and red onion salad that I love to serve it with. Alternatively, you could spoon some pesto or warm passata (puréed tomatoes) over the top. Thin pasta works best in the pie as the fine strands bind together well.

INGREDIENTS

220 g (8 oz) vermicelli, angel hair
  pasta or spaghettini
2 large eggs
50 g (1¾ oz) parmesan, grated,
  plus extra to serve if desired
2 tablespoons chopped
  flat-leaf (Italian) parsley
1 garlic clove, crushed
100 ml (3½ fl oz) milk
salt and pepper
1 tablespoon olive oil
1 tablespoon butter

TOMATO SALAD

4 large ripe tomatoes, sliced 1 cm
  (½ in) thick
½ red onion, thinly sliced
salt and pepper
1 tablespoon extra-virgin olive oil
2 teaspoons red-wine vinegar
2 tablespoons roughly chopped
  flat-leaf (Italian) parsley

HOW TO

Boil the pasta in well-salted water for a minute or so less than the packet recommends. Drain and rinse with cold water.

In a large bowl whisk the remaining ingredients except the oil and butter. Stir in the pasta until evenly combined.

Heat the oil and butter in a 25 cm (10 in) saucepan over a low–medium heat. Use a pastry brush to brush the oil up the sides of the pan. Tip in the pasta, then flatten and press it down (I do this with the bottom of a plate). Cook for around 3 minutes, then check to see if there is a golden crust developing on the base. (It's important not to burn it here or it can become bitter.) When golden, place a large plate on top of the saucepan and carefully flip the pan and plate upside down, dropping the pasta onto the plate. Slide the pasta back into the pan. Continue to cook for another 3 minutes.

While the pasta is cooking, lay the tomato slices over a plate or wide bowl and scatter on the onion. Season with salt and pepper, and drizzle with the oil and vinegar. Scatter with the parsley.

Serve the vermicelli pie with the tomato salad and some extra parmesan if desired.

GĦAĠIN GRIEG

GREEK PASTA

PREPARATION: 5 MINUTES COOKING: 20 MINUTES

The ingredients of this one-pot wonder fuse together to create a decadent bowl of warmth. Because the pasta is not boiled first, the starch remains and adds creaminess like a well-cooked risotto. A good deal of butter and parmesan help too! It's a mystery why the Maltese dish is known as 'Greek', but one theory is that it uses small pasta such as *orzo*, popular in Greece. Pork mince or Maltese sausage are traditionally used, but I like to use lamb as it's leaner. One could speculate that this recipe predates the 18th century, as it is absent of any tomato. The earliest reference to tomatoes in Malta was in 1782. Today a recipe without them is almost sacrilege.

INGREDIENTS

1 litre (34 fl oz/4 cups) chicken stock

90 g (3 oz) butter

1 onion, finely diced

1 garlic clove, finely chopped

300 g (10½ oz) lean minced
   (ground) lamb or pork

2 bacon rashers, finely chopped

salt and pepper

250 ml (8½ fl oz/1 cup)
   dry white wine

3 bay leaves

1 × 10 cm (4 in) rosemary sprig

350 g (12½ oz) small pasta such as
   ditali, ditalini, fregola, orzo or risoni

60 g (2 oz) parmesan, finely grated

3 tablespoons chopped parsley

HOW TO

Heat the stock in a saucepan until gently simmering. Meanwhile, melt the butter except for 1 tablespoon in a separate saucepan over a medium heat. Sauté the onion and garlic until soft (around 5 minutes). Add the minced meat, bacon and some salt and pepper and cook, breaking up the clumps, until the meat is lightly browned. Add the wine, bay leaves, rosemary sprig and pasta and start to cook, stirring, as you would a risotto.

When the wine is absorbed, pour in a little hot stock from the saucepan and continue to cook, stirring occasionally. Keep adding more stock until the pasta is al dente (you may not need all the stock). Remove the rosemary sprig and stir in the parmesan, chopped parsley and reserved butter. Serve with crusty bread.

Hills roll to the water's edge, spires on the horizon.
Peninsulas and ports made and defended by knights.
Women chat over hanging laundry - iconic Maltese balconies of the
most beautiful woodwork and colours.
Revellers dine and laugh at St Julian's, still within reach of that
clear Mediterranean blue.
Night swimming; all is calm while lights dance in the distance.
A quiet dawn preludes *pastizzi* and coffee. A new day in Valletta.

IMQARRUN IL-FORN
BAKED MACARONI

PREPARATION: 25 MINUTES COOKING: 1 HOUR 20 MINUTES

Imqarrun il-forn evokes memories of lunch at my grandmother's. If this wasn't on the table, it was often in the fridge. My cousins and I would fight each other over the irresistible crusty edges (which are helped along by a dusting of semolina in the baking dish). Like *Ross il-forn* (page 148), the dish is found in cafes and bakeries all over Malta and Gozo, sold in small aluminium containers for an easy lunch. The recipe is similar to *Timpana* (page 161), but less grandiose and without pastry. The exclusions make it easier to bring together any night of the week (though ingredients such as chicken livers, boiled eggs and peas can be included if you like). Baked macaroni doesn't reheat well, but I find it delicious eaten cold from the fridge on a hot summer's day.

INGREDIENTS

3 large ripe tomatoes or 400 g (14 oz)
   tinned diced tomatoes

1 onion, finely chopped

2 garlic cloves, finely chopped

2 tablespoons olive oil, plus extra
   for oiling

500 g (1 lb 2 oz) minced (ground)
   beef or pork, or a mixture

80 g (2¾ oz) bacon or pancetta,
   diced (optional)

100 ml (3½ fl oz) red wine

2 tablespoons tomato paste
   (concentrated purée)

½ teaspoon dried oregano

salt and pepper

500 g (1 lb 2 oz) macaroni (straight,
   not elbow), long tubular pasta
   (up to 25 cm/10 in) or penne

1 egg

150 ml (5 fl oz) milk

⅛ teaspoon ground nutmeg

70 g (2½ oz) parmesan, grated

2 tablespoons fine semolina

HOW TO

If using fresh tomatoes, score them on their bases and grate with a box grater. Sauté the onion and garlic with 2 tablespoons of oil in a large saucepan over a medium heat for 5 minutes. Add the minced meat and bacon or pancetta (if using) and cook until browned with any moisture evaporated. Add the wine and tomato paste and allow the wine to cook off. Now add the tomatoes, oregano and some salt and pepper. Cover with a lid and simmer for 45 minutes, adding a splash of water if the ragu becomes too dry. Taste and add extra seasoning if needed.

Meanwhile, boil the pasta in well-salted water for a few minutes less than the packet recommends. Drain and rinse with cold water.

Whisk the egg in a small bowl with the milk, nutmeg and half the parmesan. In a large mixing bowl, combine the pasta with the ragu, then add the milk mixture and stir through.

Preheat the oven to 200°C (400°F). Rub a large casserole dish with a splash of oil and sprinkle the semolina over the base and sides. Spread the pasta mixture in the dish, top with the remaining parmesan and drizzle with 1 tablespoon of oil. Cover in foil and bake for 10 minutes on the top shelf of the oven. Remove the foil and continue to bake until the top is crusty with some burnt spots. If a crust does not develop, increase the heat. Beneath the crusty surface, the pasta should remain moist.

PASTA BEAD AND BROAD BEAN SOUP
KUSKSU

<u>PREPARATION</u>: 20 MINUTES <u>COOKING</u>: 30 MINUTES

Kusksu are tiny pasta beads produced in Malta. Their size is about that of a large peppercorn. Given their similarity to couscous in shape and name, it's likely their origin dates back to the Arabic occupation of Malta, although little evidence exists. This dish is known by the same name, and includes another of Malta's favourite ingredients – fresh broad beans – plus a touch of the omnipresent tomato paste, and Malta's loved *ġbejniet* cheese. Sitting somewhere between a soup and very wet pasta, it's often served in spring when broad beans come into season, but is delightful in colder weather using frozen beans. If you can't find the pasta, look for pearl couscous or fregola (a similar toasted pasta from Sardinia), or substitute a small pasta such as ditalini.

INGREDIENTS

180 g (6½ oz) podded broad
  (fava) beans
1 medium onion, finely diced
1 garlic clove, finely sliced
2 tablespoons olive oil
2 tablespoons tomato paste
  (concentrated purée)
1 litre (34 fl oz/4 cups) vegetable
  stock or water
100 g (3½ oz) kusksu (or pearl
  couscous, fregola or ditalini pasta)
2 tablespoons chopped mint
2 tablespoons chopped
  flat-leaf (Italian) parsley
1 teaspoon salt
freshly ground black pepper
4 fresh *ġbejniet* cheeselets
  (page 46) or 360 g (12½ oz)
  firm ricotta divided into 4 pieces
50 g (1¾ oz) parmesan (or any other
  hard salty cheese), finely grated
80 g diced bacon (optional)

HOW TO

Blanch the broad beans for 3 minutes in salted boiling water, then drain, rinse briefly and tip into a bowl of iced water. Use your thumbnail to pierce the skins and pop out the beans inside.

Sauté the bacon (if using), onion and garlic with the oil in a saucepan over a medium heat until the onions are soft. Stir in the tomato paste, then add the stock or water and kusksu and bring to the boil. Simmer for 15 minutes with the lid slightly ajar. Add the broad beans and simmer for a further 5 minutes before removing from the heat. (If using pearl couscous, fregola or ditalini, check the cooking time on the packet and reduce the cooking accordingly.) Stir through the herbs, saving some for garnish, plus the salt and some pepper. Taste for seasoning.

Place a cheeselet or piece of ricotta in the middle of each bowl, then ladle the soup over the top. Scatter with the remaining herbs and grated parmesan.

RAVJUL ZALZETT MALTI

RAVIOLI WITH MALTESE SAUSAGE

PREPARATION: 40 MINUTES + RESTING COOKING: 20 MINUTES

Maltese sausages were traditionally made in a fashion to preserve the meat without refrigeration, cured for eating raw. In this ravioli recipe, I replicate the garlicky, coriander-tinged flavour of authentic Maltese sausages, but use fresh minced pork. Ravioli is commonplace on Maltese menus, often filled with ricotta. At Briju, one of my favourite restaurants in Valletta, I ate a dish similar to this, served with little flair or garnish, straight out of the pot drizzled only with extra-virgin olive oil. I thought perhaps the chef had forgotten the sauce then realised the intent was to taste the joyous marriage of Maltese sausage flavours and olive oil.

PASTA

200 g (7 oz/1⅓ cups) strong
  white flour, plus extra for dusting
150 g (5½ oz) fine semolina,
  plus extra for dusting
1 teaspoon salt
3 eggs
2 tablespoons olive oil

FILLING

500 g (1 lb 2 oz)
  minced (ground) pork
1 tablespoon coriander seeds
2 tablespoons olive oil
½ teaspoon black peppercorns
1 garlic clove
2 tablespoons finely chopped
  flat-leaf (Italian) parsley
1 teaspoon sea salt

1 egg, lightly beaten
extra-virgin olive oil, to serve

HOW TO

Combine the flour, semolina and salt in a bowl. Create a well in the middle, use a fork to whisk the eggs and oil into the flour, then use your hands to form a stiff dough. Transfer to a work surface and knead for a couple of minutes until smooth. Sprinkle with a little extra flour if the dough seems too sticky. Cover the dough with a tea towel (dish towel) and leave to rest for about 30 minutes.

Meanwhile, put the pork in a mixing bowl and allow to come to room temperature. Sauté the coriander seeds in the oil over a medium heat until fragrant. Grind the seeds and oil with the peppercorns, garlic, parsley and salt using a mortar and pestle. Mix the herb salt through the pork.

Start with a quarter of the dough, keeping the rest covered. Dust it lightly in flour, then use a rolling pin to flatten it to a rectangle about the width of your hand. Now begin to run it through a pasta machine, starting on the widest setting. Run the piece through a few times, folding in the ragged edges between each roll, until you have a smooth sheet with straight sides. Decrease the width by a notch and roll the sheet through again. Continue decreasing the width, rolling until the sheet is around 90 cm (3 ft) long. (You won't need to go to the narrowest setting, keeping the pasta a little thicker.) Set the pasta sheet aside and roll out a second piece of dough.

Dollop heaped teaspoons of filling 8 cm (3¼ in) apart across 1 pasta sheet. Brush beaten egg around each mound of filling. Lay the second sheet over the top and gently press the sheets together around the mounds. Avoid creating pockets of air. Use an 8 cm (3¼ in) round cutter to cut ravioli. Dust a baking tray with semolina and lightly coat each ravioli. Repeat with the remaining dough and filling. Pasta scraps can be cut, tossed with semolina and stored in the freezer for later.

Bring 4 litres (135 fl oz/16 cups) of well-salted water to a gentle simmer and add a quarter of the ravioli. Simmer for 4 minutes, remove with a slotted spoon into bowls. Continue cooking the ravioli in batches. Drizzle with extra-virgin olive oil to serve.

SPAGHETTI WITH BOTTARGA AND BREADCRUMBS

<u>PREPARATION</u>: 15 MINUTES <u>COOKING</u>: 20 MINUTES

Bottarga is the cured roe pouch of grey mullet, synonymous with Sardinia and Sicily. But it is also used in other parts of the Mediterranean including Malta, where tuna bottarga is more common and has a stronger taste. When salted and dried, the roe develops a deep umami flavour. Grated, it can also be served on bread with fresh tomato, or put in salads. I love how easy this dish is to prepare. The key to its success is emulsifying the pasta water and oil to give a creaminess. The fried breadcrumbs add texture.

BREADCRUMBS

150 g (5½ oz) stale continental-style
   bread, roughly cut or torn
2 tablespoons olive oil
1 tablespoon butter
salt and pepper

INGREDIENTS

120 ml (4 fl oz) olive oil
2 garlic cloves, lightly bruised
¼ teaspoon dried chilli flakes
40 g (1½ oz) bottarga (dried mullet
   or tuna roe), finely grated
   (as you would citrus zest)
350 g (12½ oz) long pasta such as
   spaghetti, spaghettoni or linguine
2 tablespoons finely chopped
   flat-leaf (Italian) parsley
grated zest of 1 lemon
1 tablespoon lemon juice

HOW TO

Blitz the bread in a food processor, stopping before the crumbs become too fine, allowing them to be slightly irregular. Fry them in a frying pan with the oil and butter until golden brown. Season with salt and pepper, then scoop onto a plate lined with paper towel.

Heat the oil and garlic together in the pan over a medium heat, turning the garlic often. Once the garlic has infused the oil and is lightly golden, remove it. Add the chilli and cook for 30 seconds, then add most of the bottarga (reserving 2 tablespoons for garnish), letting it melt into the oil. Remove the pan from the heat.

While you are cooking the garlic, chilli and bottarga, boil the pasta in well-salted water as directed on the packet. Before draining, scoop out 375 ml (12½ fl oz/1½ cups) of the cooking water.

Gently reheat the pan of bottarga oil and add 125 ml (4 fl oz/½ cup) of cooking water. Toss the hot pasta through the oil, mixing to emulsify the water and oil. Add more splashes of water as needed until you have a wet, creamy consistency. Add the parsley, lemon zest and juice and mix until well combined. Divide between 4 bowls and top with the remaining bottarga. Sprinkle with the breadcrumbs.

SEAFOOD

As the Maltese appreciation of fish continues to increase, so too does the diversity of seafood on offer and the methods of its preparation.

Wherever you are in Malta, you are within minutes of the sea. But for a long time, the Maltese kept to minimal fish varieties, and the islands' consumption of seafood wasn't at the levels you would expect of a nation engulfed by salt water. Common varieties included John Dory, grouper, hake, lampuki and amberjack as well as octopus and calamari.

Traditionally, seafood was considered more of an everyday or peasant food, and weekend or celebratory meals were dominated by meat and vegetables. But as the Maltese appreciation of fish continues to increase, so too does the diversity of seafood on offer and the methods of its preparation.

In the old days, one would hear the call of fish sellers on Wednesdays and Fridays, yelling 'friski u ħajjin' ('fresh and alive') as they entered town. Today seafood is rife in markets, at roadside stalls and on dinner tables.

Unlike in some parts of Europe, fishermen are still able to make a living from the sea. In Marsaxlokk, south of Valletta, the harbour boasts many colourful fishing boats known as luzzu, adorned with carved and painted eyes on their bows. Superstition suggests these eyes protect the fishermen in their perilous profession – an industry that dates as far back as the Phoenicians who arrived in Malta over 2000 years ago. Marsaxlokk has a market each Sunday, when locals and tourists descend on the town to browse the fruits of the Mediterranean.

This chapter includes classic Maltese preparations, as well as some inspired by island ingredients and the bounty of the surrounding sea.

QARNIT BIT-TEWM
OCTOPUS SALAD

PREPARATION: 20 MINUTES COOKING: 40 MINUTES + RESTING AND CHILLING

This cold salad is perfect for a hot day in the sun or as an appetiser. Pair it with some fresh *ħobż* and you have a refreshing and delicious light meal. The vinegar should come through strongly. Any leftovers can be kept in the refrigerator for a few days.

INGREDIENTS

1 small octopus weighing about
  600 g (1 lb 5 oz)
1 teaspoon salt
3 tablespoons extra-virgin olive oil
1 garlic clove, thinly sliced
freshly ground black pepper
2 tablespoons white-wine or
  sherry vinegar
1 red onion, thinly sliced
100 g (3½ oz) cherry or grape
  tomatoes, halved
1 large handful basil leaves
1 large handful flat-leaf
  (Italian) parsley leaves,
  roughly chopped
lemon wedges, to serve

HOW TO

To clean the octopus, cut between the head and tentacles just below the eyes. Cut a slice from the bottom of the head including the eyes and discard. Insert your knife into the head and make a slit in order to open it up. Pull out the contents of the head, then peel off the outer skin. Push out the beak in the centre of the tentacles and discard. Rinse the head and tentacles.

Bring the octopus to the boil in a medium saucepan of water with the salt added. Once simmering, cook for 35 minutes with the lid on. Turn off the heat and leave the octopus in the water for another 40 minutes with the lid ajar.

Remove the octopus from the water and cut into small pieces of around 3 cm (1¼ in). Heat 1 tablespoon of the oil in a frying pan over a low heat and sauté the garlic for 1 minute. Add the octopus pieces and some pepper and increase the heat to medium. Now add the vinegar and toss to combine. Check the seasoning and add a dash more vinegar if you like (the flavour will be more subtle when chilled). Remove from the heat and toss through another tablespoon of the oil.

Transfer the octopus to a bowl and leave to cool, then chill in the refrigerator. Once cold, add the onion, tomatoes and herbs and toss together. Check the seasoning again and scoop onto a sharing plate. Drizzle with the remaining oil. Serve with the lemon wedges and small forks or toothpicks. The octopus goes well with crusty bread, and can even be packed in a container for the beach (if kept cold).

ALJOTTA
GARLIC FISH SOUP

PREPARATION: 25 MINUTES COOKING: 45 MINUTES

This traditional broth has a delicate consistency but packs a punch, concentrating some of Malta's most loved flavours: fish, tomatoes and garlic (and also including a small amount of rice). The name '*aljotta*' comes from '*aglio*', the Italian word for garlic, so don't be scared to go heavy with it! No actual fish should be served in the broth – it is in the soup purely to flavour it. I've met fishermen on the shore presenting a bucket of small fish as the day's catch, saying 'It's okay, I can make *aljotta*!' Any fresh fish can be used, but especially 'cheap' fish and fish heads. Because the soup is strained, you don't even need to scale the fish. Plenty of fresh mint and marjoram or parsley are essential.

INGREDIENTS

500 g (1 lb 2 oz) ripe tomatoes

1 large onion, chopped

3 tablespoons olive oil

6 garlic cloves, finely sliced

2 tablespoons tomato paste
 (concentrated purée)

6 small fish (about 600 g/1 lb 5 oz),
 cleaned – sardines are perfect, or
 use heads, tails and trimmings
 of larger fish

3 tablespoons chopped mint

3 tablespoons chopped marjoram
 or flat-leaf (Italian) parsley

1 litre (34 fl oz/4 cups) water

salt and pepper

75 g (2¾ oz/⅓ cup) short-grain rice

juice of ½ lemon, plus wedges
 to serve

HOW TO

Score the tomatoes on their bases and grate with a box grater. Fry the onion in the oil in a large saucepan. When translucent, add the garlic and continue to fry until golden. Add the tomatoes, tomato paste, fish and half of the herbs. Stir for a minute, then add the water and some salt and pepper. Simmer for 30 minutes with the lid on.

Pass the soup through a mouli (food mill) into a clean saucepan, pressing until only fish skin and dry bones remain. Alternatively, press through a fine sieve with a large spoon.

Bring the broth back to the boil. Add the rice, stir well, and cook until the rice is tender. Remove the soup from the heat and add the remaining herbs and lemon juice. Serve with more lemon wedges and lots of crusty bread.

SALT-CURED TUNA, ROMANO BEANS, PRESERVED LEMON

PREPARATION: 20 MINUTES + 3 DAYS CURING   COOKING: 10 MINUTES

This is a great way to enhance the flavour of tuna while also extending its shelf life. Preserved this way, the fish is similar to salmon gravlax, but tuna has a denser texture and there is also less sugar in the cure, making it more savoury. The tuna is often used in a Gozitan pie of pumpkin (winter squash), rice and green olives, but it can be used any number of ways – through pasta with fresh tomato, onion and garlic, for example. The preserved lemon added to this dish offsets the umami of the tuna and makes the beans sing.

SALT-CURED TUNA

200 g (7 oz) salt
40 g (1½ oz) sugar
2 tuna steaks (total 300 g/10½ oz)
approximately 200 ml (7 fl oz)
  extra-virgin olive oil

INGREDIENTS

2 shallots, finely diced
1 tablespoon olive oil
500 g (1 lb 2 oz) flat (romano) beans,
  or green beans, ends trimmed
¼ preserved lemon, flesh discarded,
  thinly sliced
1 tsp chilli flakes (optional)

HOW TO

Make the tuna at least 3 days in advance. Put a third of the salt and sugar in the base of a wide glass jar. Lay the first tuna steak in the jar, and follow with another third of the salt and sugar. Repeat these layers, then press down gently on the salt-covered fish. Put a lid on the jar and refrigerate for 2 days.

Rinse the fish and pat it dry. Dice it into 1 cm (½ in) pieces and place in a clean jar. Cover with the oil and refrigerate for at least 1 more day.

Remove 2 heaped tablespoons of tuna from the jar and place on a chopping board (the remaining tuna can be stored in the refrigerator for another dish). Finely dice the tuna.

Sauté the shallots in the oil in a frying pan over a medium heat until soft and translucent. Meanwhile, blanch the beans in salted boiling water for a few minutes until bright green. Drain and add to the frying pan. Add the tuna, preserved lemon and chilli flakes, if using, and gently toss it all together. Taste for seasoning and serve.

PULPETTI TAT-TONN

TUNA FISHCAKES

PREPARATION: 20 MINUTES COOKING: 30 MINUTES

Fishcake recipes are always handy, featuring ingredients from the pantry. In Malta, similar patties are also made with corned beef. I like to serve these with plenty of lemon and a salad of iceberg lettuce. They are also nice eaten cold and can be added to a *platt Malti.*

INGREDIENTS

600 g (1 lb 5 oz) potatoes,
  peeled and halved if large
2 eggs
2 medium tins tuna in oil
  (approximately 350 g/12½ oz),
  drained
1 tablespoon chopped mint
1 tablespoon chopped
  flat-leaf (Italian) parsley
2 tablespoons chopped spring
  onion (scallion)
salt and pepper
80 ml (2½ fl oz/⅓ cup) milk
75 g (2¾ oz/½ cup) plain
  (all-purpose) flour
100 g (3½ oz/1 cup) dry breadcrumbs
neutral oil for frying such as
  sunflower or canola
1 lemon, cut into wedges to serve

HOW TO

Bring a large saucepan of well-salted water to the boil. Add the potatoes and cook until soft (about 15 minutes). Drain then place in a large bowl and allow to dry out and cool down until you are able to handle them. Grate the potatoes into the bowl using a box grater.

Whisk 1 of the eggs and add to the potatoes along with the tuna, herbs, spring onions and some salt and pepper. Stir to combine.

Whisk the remaining egg and milk in a bowl. Put the flour and breadcrumbs onto separate plates. Shape the tuna and potato mixture into balls slightly larger than golf balls and flatten into patties. Roll in flour, then egg, then breadcrumbs.

Pour a generous layer of oil into a frying pan to use for shallow frying. Heat the pan, then fry the patties in a few batches until golden on each side. Drain on paper towel before serving with the lemon wedges.

SWORDFISH CARPACCIO

PREPARATION: 25 MINUTES COOKING: 5 MINUTES

Swordfish in Malta is often baked in the oven with a splash of wine and garlic, but personally I find this method doesn't do justice to such a beautiful fish, as the result is often a little dry. I prefer to serve it raw in this carpaccio, topped with fried capers and segments of pink grapefruit. If you don't like raw fish, the recipe gives you the option to cure it in the dressing, or you could even grill the swordfish (see below).

INGREDIENTS

1 × 350–400 g (12½–14 oz) thick
  swordfish fillet
2 tablespoons olive or vegetable oil
  for frying
2 tablespoons extra-virgin olive oil
  for serving
3 tablespoons capers, rinsed and
  patted dry
1 large pink grapefruit
salt and pepper
1 tablespoon chopped
  flat-leaf (Italian) parsley

GRILLED SWORDFISH
WITH PINK GRAPEFRUIT

Take 2 swordfish steaks and grill them for a few minutes on one side (depending on their thickness). Flip the steaks onto a plate and prepare the salad. By the time you serve them with the salad, the fish should have just cooked through with the meat flaking apart. If you want to cook more swordfish steaks, just increase the amount of grapefruit and other ingredients.

HOW TO

Freeze the fish, as this makes thin slicing easier and also kills any bacteria that may be present. I advise you to do this (though it's not strictly necessary).

Heat the 2 tablespoons of frying oil in a saucepan over medium-high heat. Add the capers and fry until crisp and lightly brown. Scoop onto paper towel to drain.

Grate the zest of half the grapefruit into a mixing bowl. Use a small sharp knife to slice off the skin of the fruit just beyond the pith. You will see white vertical lines around the fruit. Make an incision either side of these, slicing towards the core to remove the segments. Cut each segment into thirds, creating little wedges. Put the grapefruit in a small bowl. Tip any accumulated juice into the bowl of zest, along with the remaining tablespoon of oil.

With a large sharp knife, cut the swordfish by turning the fillets on their side and slicing as thinly as possible. Add the fish to the bowl of dressing. If you enjoy raw fish, just mix the fish with the dressing and serve immediately. Alternatively, let the fish steep in the dressing for up to 30 minutes, which will make it more like a ceviche.

Lay the slices of fish across 4 plates. Season with salt and pepper, then top with the grapefruit segments, fried capers and parsley. Drizzle with a little more oil. Serve with crusty bread.

SERVES 6

SPINACH AND TUNA PIE

PREPARATION: 45 MINUTES COOKING: 50 MINUTES

The Maltese haven't taken to tuna in the same manner as the Japanese, Peruvians or even the Italians. In Malta, tuna is not appreciated raw – but the highly versatile product that is tinned tuna finds its way into salads, fishcakes (page 119) and pies like this one. I love how this rustic, wholesome pie can also be eaten cold. For a far superior taste and consistency, I implore you to use a bunch of spinach rather than baby spinach leaves. There's a bit more work involved in the preparation, but it's worth it. Also try to use a quality sustainable tinned tuna in oil.

SHORTCRUST PASTRY

300 g (10½ oz/2 cups) plain (all-purpose) flour, plus extra for dusting
½ teaspoon dried mint
½ teaspoon salt
140 g (5 oz) butter, chilled and diced, plus extra for greasing
50–60 ml (1¾–2 fl oz) iced water

FILLING

1 large onion, finely chopped
1 garlic clove, finely chopped
1 tablespoon olive oil
400 g (14 oz) English spinach, roots removed, chopped smaller at the stem end, larger at the leaf end
salt and pepper
2 eggs
260 g (9 oz) drained tinned tuna
3 tablespoons olives of any variety, pitted and chopped
2 tablespoons chopped mint
80 g (2¾ oz) peas, rinsed if frozen

1 egg, beaten
sesame seeds, to sprinkle

HOW TO

Combine the flour, mint and salt in a large bowl. Add the butter and rub together with your fingers until the mixture resembles breadcrumbs or rough sand. Add the cold water bit by bit and work in with your hands until a dough has formed (aiming not to overwork your dough). Cover in plastic wrap and chill for at least 45 minutes.

To make the filling, sauté the onion and garlic in the oil in a large frying pan over a medium heat until translucent (5 minutes). Add the spinach and some salt and pepper and cook until the spinach has wilted and is vibrant green. Tip the spinach and onion mixture into a colander to drain and cool. Squeeze the excess water out of the spinach.

Whisk the eggs in a large bowl and add the tuna, olives, mint, peas and spinach. Stir well.

Preheat the oven to 180°C (360°F) and butter a non-stick springform cake tin. Divide the dough into 2 balls, one a third bigger than the other. Roll the larger ball out on a lightly floured surface until 5 mm (¼ in) thick. Line the tin with the pastry, then scoop in the filling. Roll out the second ball of pastry and lay on top of the pie. Trim off the excess pastry leaving a small border. Fold in and use a thumb to make decorative indentations around the edge. Prick some holes in the top with a fork. Gently brush the beaten egg over the top of the pie, then sprinkle generously with sesame seeds. Bake for 35 minutes, then run a knife around the edge of the pie, remove the springform sides and return to the oven. Cook for another 10 minutes, until lightly golden.

Postcard #03

Park where you can or want.
Watch old men in older boats navigate under the cliffs.
Northerners bronze and burn in tidal pools and shallow baths,
yet solitude is minutes away.
Clamber over the rocks to another cove, the water even clearer.
Endless swimming; the appetite grows.
Dine alongside gregarious locals at the restaurant.
Grilled fish, lemon, espresso - I'll take the same tomorrow, thanks!
An evening walk along the cliffs; the gentle breeze gone, the sun
quickly dipping.
A beautiful glow, the wafting scent of wildflowers, silence on the
limestone coast.

KLAMARI MIMLIJA

STUFFED SQUID

PREPARATION: 30 MINUTES COOKING: 55 MINUTES

Stuffing calamari is a great way to use up old *ħobż* (bread). Looking at the ingredients list, this dish really is a marriage of typical Maltese produce. While gently simmering in the tomato sauce, the stuffing absorbs the flavour of the sea, pairing it with other ingredients in the filling. Mix and edit the stuffing ingredients of anchovies, olives and capers as you like using the base of bread and eggs to bind it.

SAUCE

2 large ripe tomatoes
1 small onion, finely diced
2 garlic cloves, finely chopped
1 tablespoon olive oil
200 ml (7 fl oz) white wine
salt and pepper

STUFFED SQUID

2 large squid weighing about
  550 g (1 lb 3 oz) each
3 eggs (2 of them hard-boiled,
  peeled and chopped)
1 cup (loosely packed) torn
  bread without crusts from
  a continental-style loaf
60 g (2 oz/⅓ cup) chopped
  kalamata olives
1 tablespoon capers,
  rinsed and chopped
2 anchovy fillets, finely chopped
grated zest of 1 small lemon
2 tablespoons chopped
  flat-leaf (Italian) parsley
100 ml (3½ fl oz) milk (if required)
salt and pepper

HOW TO

To make the sauce, score the tomatoes on their bases and grate with a box grater. In a large saucepan over a medium heat, fry the onion and garlic in the oil for 5 minutes until soft. Add the wine and reduce it for 3 minutes, then stir in the grated tomato and some salt and pepper, and turn off the heat.

To clean a squid, gently pull the tentacles away from the body; the intestines should come at the same time. Cut beneath the eyes to remove the intestines from the tentacles, then push out the beak in the centre of the tentacles. Pull out the transparent quill from inside the body. Slice the wings off the body. Peel the skin from the body and wings. Rinse the tentacles, wings and tube inside and out. Dice the tentacles and wings to include in the stuffing.

Crack the 1 raw egg into a large bowl and whisk. Mix in the diced squid and remaining ingredients.

Milk can be added after combining bread with the other ingredients. If the bread doesn't moisten enough with oil and vinegar from the capers, some teaspoons of milk will help soften the mixture. Stuff into the squid tubes, making sure the filling is not too loose but also not too compact, as it will expand and can split the tubes during cooking.

Reheat the pan of sauce. Scrape the sauce to the sides so that when you add the squid, it touches the pan. Lightly brown the squid tubes on two sides. Return the sauce around the squid and mix in 100 ml (3½ fl oz) of water. Cover with a lid and simmer over a very low heat for 40 minutes, adding more splashes of water if the sauce dries out.

Slice each squid tube on an angle into 4–5 pieces each. Serve the slices with the sauce, together with crusty bread and a salad or side dish.

LAMPUKI PIE

PREPARATION: 45 MINUTES COOKING: 1 HOUR 30 MINUTES

This is no humble fish pie, rather centuries of diversity on a plate, and a certified Maltese classic. In my opinion, if we were to define Malta by a single recipe, it would be this one. British pastry encases an Italian-style preparation of tomatoes, vegetables, olives, capers and Malta's beloved *lampuki* fish (mahi mahi), all finished with the flavours of mint, lemon zest and sultanas for some exotic punch. When *lampuki* is in season, some cooks make multiple pies to freeze for later.

SHORTCRUST PASTRY

See page 124

FILLING

1 × 1 kg (2 lb 3 oz) piece of mahi mahi
  (or another firm-fleshed fish such as
  marlin)
plain (all-purpose) flour, for coating
salt and pepper
olive oil, for frying
1 small or ½ large cauliflower
  (600 g/1 lb 5 oz), cut into florets
600 g (1 lb 5 oz) English spinach
2 large ripe tomatoes
  (about 300 g/10½ oz)
1 large onion, diced
100 g (3½ oz/¾ cup) baby peas,
  rinsed if frozen
2 tablespoons tomato paste
  (concentrated purée)
2 tablespoons capers, rinsed
1 tablespoon sultanas,
  (golden raisins) chopped
12 black olives, pitted and chopped
3 tablespoons chopped
  flat-leaf (Italian) parsley
1 teaspoon dried mint
grated zest of ½ lemon
½ teaspoon ground allspice

HOW TO

Make the pastry as per the recipe on page 124.

Cut the fish into slices through the bones, discarding the tail if included. Put some flour onto a plate and season with salt and pepper, stirring. Coat the fish pieces in the seasoned flour. Heat a generous layer of oil in a frying pan and fry the fish on each side until just cooked through. Drain on paper towel. When cool enough to handle, carefully remove the skin and bones and cut into bite-sized pieces. Set aside.

Boil the cauliflower florets until tender (about 12 minutes), then drain and refresh in cold water. Slice off the spinach roots, then wash and drain the leaves. Remove the excess water by tipping onto a clean tea towel (dish towel) and patting dry. Chop smaller at the stem end, larger at the leaf end.

Sauté spinach in a pan with oil until it wilts, transfer to a strainer and squeeze out excess water. Score the tomatoes on their bases and grate with a box grater. Fry the onion in a little oil in a saucepan until soft and translucent, then add the tomatoes and cook for 1 minute. Combine the cauliflower and cooked tomato, onion and spinach in a large bowl. Add the remaining ingredients (except the fish). Season with salt and pepper and mix well.

Preheat the oven to 180°C (360°F) and butter a large non-stick springform cake tin. Divide the dough into 2 balls, one a third bigger than the other. Roll the larger ball out on a lightly floured surface to 5 mm (¼ in) thick. Line the tin with the pastry. Spread half the vegetable mixture over the pastry base, then scatter the fried fish pieces evenly over the top. Cover with the remaining vegetables. Roll out the second ball of pastry and lay over the top of the pie. Trim off the excess pastry leaving a small border. Fold in and use a thumb to make decorative indentations around the edge. Prick the lid all over with a fork. Bake in the oven for 45 minutes, then run a knife around the edge of the pie, remove the springform sides and cook for another 15 minutes. Allow the pie to sit for 10 minutes before serving.

PULPETTI TAL-MAKKU

WHITEBAIT FRITTERS

PREPARATION: 10 MINUTES COOKING: 10 MINUTES

Small school fish are caught in shallow bays around Malta using hand-held seine nets. Floats keep the nets up on the surface, so the method doesn't damage the seabed like trawlers. It's a preferred fishing technique that I hope Malta holds on to. These fritters traditionally contain onion and garlic, but I like to taste only the fish with a fresh dash of lemon and herbs, so I leave them out (but you can add if you like). While the fritters are usually cooked in a frying pan in the kitchen, they can easily be cooked on a flat barbecue near the beach or by the pool – they are beautiful on a hot day. Serve them with a green salad, or the White bean salad (page 39). The recipe makes four fritters, but you can make them smaller if you want to serve as an appetiser.

INGREDIENTS

250 g (9 oz) whitebait

2 tablespoons cornflour (cornstarch)
  or plain (all-purpose) flour

1 egg plus 2 egg whites

grated zest of ½ lemon

1 tablespoon finely chopped mint
  or flat-leaf (Italian) parsley

½ teaspoon salt

freshly ground black pepper

80 ml (2½ fl oz/⅓ cup) sunflower,
  peanut or canola oil

lemon wedges, to serve

HOW TO

Combine the whitebait and flour in a mixing bowl and toss until the fish is evenly coated.

Separate the whole egg and whisk the yolk in a small bowl. Beat the 3 egg whites in a separate bowl to firm peaks.

Stir the egg yolk through the whitebait, then fold in the egg whites, lemon zest, herbs, salt and some pepper.

Heat half the oil in a frying pan over a medium heat. Use a large spoon to scoop a quarter of the mixture into one side of the pan. Add another scoop to the other side. Cook the fritters for a couple of minutes on each side, until lightly golden. Drain the fritters on paper towels while you continue to cook the remaining 2 fritters with the remaining oil. Serve with lemon wedges.

LAMPUKI WITH TOMATO CAPER SAUCE

PREPARATION: 15 MINUTES COOKING: 15 MINUTES

Lampuki is the Maltese name for a fish also known as mahi mahi, dorado or dolphin fish. Caught between August and December, huge schools head north in the Mediterranean. Maltese fishermen arrange rafts of palm leaves in their assigned zones in an attempt to attract the fish, who like to hide underneath from the sun. The practice is never far from drama as families have been known to enter territorial wars over *lampuki* fishing rights, and poachers from Tunisia are proving a threat.

The famed fish pie (page 131) is made when *lampuki* is in abundance. This is another delicious traditional dish of fried *lampuki* with a tomato and caper sauce, which is a subtle play on sweet and sour. Serve it with green beans or other greens, crusty bread and white wine.

SAUCE

3 large ripe tomatoes
1 tablespoon olive oil
3 garlic cloves, finely chopped
50 g (1¾ oz/⅓ cup) capers,
  rinsed and patted dry
1 teaspoon sugar
1 tablespoon chopped
  flat-leaf (Italian) parsley
1 tablespoon chopped mint
60 g (2 oz/½ cup) pitted black olives
  such as kalamata or niçoise
2 teaspoons white-wine vinegar
freshly ground black pepper

INGREDIENTS

4 × 150 g (5½ oz) fillets of mahi mahi
  (or another firm-fleshed fish such
  as marlin)
salt and pepper
75 g (2¾ oz/½ cup) plain
  (all-purpose) flour
1 tablespoon olive oil
1 tablespoon butter
lemon wedges, to serve

HOW TO

Score the tomatoes on their bases and grate with a box grater. Heat the oil in a saucepan over a medium heat and fry the garlic until just browned. Add the capers and fry for 1 minute, then add the tomatoes and sugar. Stir well, cover with a lid and heat until the sauce begins to simmer. Uncover, lower the heat and simmer for about 8 minutes, adding a splash of water if needed. The tomatoes will collapse and the sauce should have a thick but wet consistency. Finally add the herbs, olives, vinegar and a little pepper, mixing well. Check the seasoning. Reheat the sauce just before serving.

Season the fish fillets with salt and pepper before lightly coating with the flour. Heat the oil and butter in a frying pan over a medium heat. Add the fish and cook for around 3–4 minutes on the first side, then turn. Continue to cook until the centre of the fish is opaque. (Check by inserting a sharp-tipped knife into a fish fillet and peering inside; the exact cooking time depends on the thickness of your fish.) Serve immediately with the hot sauce and lemon wedges.

GANDOFFLI, ŻAGĦFRAN, BUŻBIEŻ
CLAMS WITH SAFFRON AND FENNEL

PREPARATION: 10 MINUTES COOKING: 15 MINUTES

A relative of saffron called the yellow-throated crocus (*Crocus longiflorus*) grows on Malta. It is not nearly as famous as *Crocus sativus*, but still fragrant and colourful. But the families who know where to find it are unlikely to divulge any information!

Wild fennel is a little easier to come across. In this dish, fennel seeds, saffron, wine and clams marry to make one of the most divine broths that *ħobż* (crusty white bread) ever had the pleasure to dive into.

INGREDIENTS

1 teaspoon fennel seeds
50 g (1¾ oz) butter
½ large fennel bulb
  (about 200 g/7 oz), finely diced
2 small shallots, finely diced
1 generous pinch of saffron threads
150 ml (5 fl oz) dry white wine
1 kg (2 lb 3 oz) medium-sized clams
  (*vongole*)
2 tablespoons finely chopped
  flat-leaf (Italian) parsley

HOW TO

Toast the fennel seeds in a medium saucepan over a medium heat until fragrant. Add the butter, diced fennel and shallots and sauté for 5–8 minutes, until soft and translucent. Meanwhile, mix the saffron with the wine in a glass.

Increase the heat of the pan to high and add the clams. Stir them around with the fennel and shallots, then pour in the wine and saffron. Cover with a lid and cook for 3–5 minutes. Once the clams have opened, remove the lid, stir in the parsley, reduce the heat and simmer for a minute longer. Serve with bread and salad.

MEAT

With the sweltering Mediterranean summers, you would not expect some of Malta's most beloved dishes to be hearty winter warmers.

Dishes like Beef olives (page 156), countless other stews, pies and pasta bakes are frequently consumed in Malta. I speculate it's the novelty of the short winters, and the fact that some of these dishes are often eaten on special occasions, that gives them their profound place in the hearts of the Maltese.

Lush green pastures are a tall order on the limestone islands, so beef consumption is low. Pork is more commonly farmed and appears in more recipes. The iconic Maltese pork sausage is traditionally consumed in its raw cured form, once absolutely swimming in salt to ensure it travelled well for shepherds. Today many people prefer it cooked (and less salty).

One thing to note about meat consumption in Malta is how little chicken is eaten. Aside from restaurant menus catering for tourists, it rarely appears in traditional recipes, and until recently it wasn't common in the home kitchen.

Rabbit, on the other hand, is farmed to satisfy Malta's unequivocal appreciation of the meat, and rabbit stew is crowned Malta's national dish. Horse meat is still on menus in some restaurants, but faces extinction – enjoyed by French visitors, scolded by the Brits. It's usually cooked slowly in a stew to tenderise it. Quail are another common wild meat now bred for consumption, and the Maltese appreciate snails.

BEBBUX MIMLI

SNAILS IN HERB AND TOMATO BROTH

PREPARATION: 15 MINUTES + 10 DAYS PURGING COOKING: 20 MINUTES

Like their North African neighbours, the Maltese enjoy snails. They are low in fat and high in protein, their earthiness carries other flavours well, and their texture is surprisingly pleasant. They are prepared in autumn after the first rains, when typical garden snails appear in the rocks and grass. Snails then pop up in grocery stores, traditional restaurants and sports bars. Some recipes involve boiling in beer or diluted sea water, then finishing in a tomato-based sauce. I like to simmer them in white wine with a touch of tomato and fresh herbs.

This recipe shows you how to prepare common garden snails for the table. It's important to follow the fasting and purging process to remove any toxins that the snails may have ingested. This takes ten days, so snails are not a fast food (but of course, skip this part if you can source fresh or frozen farmed snails).

INGREDIENTS

1 kg (2 lb 3 oz) brown garden snails
2 carrots
2 shallots, finely chopped
3 garlic cloves, finely chopped
2 bay leaves
50 g (1¾ oz) butter
1 tablespoon tomato paste
  (concentrated purée)
200 ml (7 fl oz) white wine
1 teaspoon chopped thyme
salt and pepper
2 tablespoons chopped
  flat-leaf (Italian) parsley

HOW TO

Put the snails in a large ventilated container with a lid and store outside or in your laundry. Purge the snails for 1 week, cleaning the container daily (to do this, tip the snails into another container while you rinse their container out, working quickly so no snails escape).

Now feed the snails with some grated carrot for 2 days; they will purge, so you will need to keep cleaning the container daily.

On the 10th day (or if using farmed snails), rinse the snails well in cold water, then boil in salted water for 5 minutes. Drain, rinse again, and soak the cooked snails in cold water for 10 minutes to remove any slimy substance.

Sauté the shallots, garlic and bay leaves with the butter in a large saucepan over a medium heat, cooking until the shallots are soft. Stir in the tomato paste, then add the wine and thyme. Bring to the boil and allow the liquid to reduce for 4 minutes. Season with salt and pepper and stir in the snails. Cook for a further 4 minutes, then remove from the heat and stir in the parsley. Serve with toothpicks to extract the meat from the shells, and enjoy with crusty bread.

KAWLATA

PORK AND VEGETABLE SOUP

PREPARATION: 25 MINUTES COOKING: 1 HOUR 15 MINUTES + 1 HOUR RESTING

Enriched with pork, this half-soup, half-stew is a winter warmer that I return to often. You can include different vegetables such as pattypan squash or zucchini (courgette). Traditionally a starch would not be added, but I find a small amount of pasta or rice helps make the dish more fulfilling. I like to let the soup sit for an hour after cooking, allowing the vegetable and pork flavours to meld together, before reheating.

INGREDIENTS

1 teaspoon fennel seeds

1 tablespoon olive oil

600 g (1 lb 5 oz) pork chops, or collar or shoulder sliced in thick steaks

1 onion, finely diced

2 carrots, diced

2 celery stalks, finely diced

1 smoked pork hock (knuckle) – about 400 g (14 oz) – or 2 large Italian pork sausages, quartered

300 g (10½ oz) choko (chayote), peeled and cut into 5 cm (2 in) chunks

300 g (10½ oz) pumpkin (winter squash), peeled, seeded and cut into 5 cm (2 in) chunks

300 g (10½ oz) white cabbage, cut into 1 cm (½ in) slices

300 g (10½ oz) potatoes, peeled and cut into 3 cm (1¼ in) chunks

2 tablespoons tomato paste (concentrated purée)

about 1.5 litres (51 fl oz/6 cups) vegetable stock or water

salt and pepper

50 g (1¾ oz) pasta such as kusksu or short vermicelli, or rice (optional)

60 g (2 oz) parmesan or ricotta salata, finely grated, to serve

HOW TO

In a heavy-based pot, gently sizzle the fennel seeds in the oil over a low heat. Add the pork chops, collar or shoulder and brown for around 3 minutes on each side. Remove the meat from the pan and add the onion, carrot and celery and sauté for about 5 minutes. Add the hock or sausage pieces and brown gently. Return the pork to the pot, along with the remaining vegetables, tomato paste and enough stock or water to cover. Bring to the boil, then gently simmer covered with a lid for 1 hour.

Turn off the heat and allow the soup to sit for 1 hour. During this time, take out the pork and hock, if using, and set aside until cool enough to handle. Remove the hock from the bone and discard the skin. Dice all the meat into 2 cm (¾ in) pieces and return to the pot.

Reheat the soup and season to taste with salt and pepper. If using pasta or rice, add to the soup and cook according to the time on the packet. Serve in bowls topped with the parmesan or ricotta salata, with plenty of crusty bread.

ROSS IL-FORN

BAKED RICE

<u>PREPARATION</u>: 20 MINUTES <u>COOKING</u>: 1 HOUR

Like a pasta bake with rice, this is the ultimate in comfort food. Not only cooked in homes, it's found throughout Malta in bakeries and snack bars sold in small foil containers. If for some outlandish reason you ever have leftovers, the dish doesn't reheat well, but is delicious cold (just like baked pasta).

Every Maltese family has their own recipe for *ross il-forn*. Some add Maltese sausage or corned beef (the tinned product is a hangover from wartimes). I've kept my recipe more Mediterranean in flavour, spicing it up with a touch of oregano and mint. An old recipe I found also calls for saffron so when I have some, I include it. Serve with crusty bread and a green salad.

INGREDIENTS

3 large ripe tomatoes or 400 g
  (14 oz) tinned diced tomatoes
500 g (1 lb 2 oz) minced (ground)
  meat (half each of beef and pork,
  or all beef)
3 tablespoons olive oil
1 large onion, finely diced
2 garlic cloves, finely chopped
100 g (3½ oz) bacon, thinly sliced
2 tablespoons tomato paste
  (concentrated purée)
500 ml (17 fl oz/2 cups) chicken stock
1½ teaspoon salt
½ teaspoon dried mint
½ teaspoon dried oregano
1 pinch of saffron threads (optional)
350 g (12½ oz/1¾ cups)
  long-grain rice
2 eggs
100 ml (3½ fl oz) milk
60 g (2 oz) parmesan, grated
3 tablespoons fresh breadcrumbs

HOW TO

If using fresh tomatoes, score them on their bases and grate with a box grater. Sauté the minced meat with 1 tablespoon of the oil in a medium saucepan over a medium–high heat until browned with any moisture evaporated. Transfer to a bowl. Add the onion, garlic and bacon to the pan and sauté over a low–medium heat until the onion is soft (around 8 minutes). Stir in the tomatoes, tomato paste, stock, salt, dried herbs and saffron (if using) and cook for 5 minutes. Add the browned meat, cover with a lid and simmer for a further 10 minutes. Turn off the heat and allow to cool.

Bring a large saucepan of salted water to the boil and cook the rice for three-quarters of the time indicated on the packet. Drain and rinse with cold water to cool the rice down.

Preheat the oven to 190°C (375°F) and butter a deep baking dish. Now enjoy the simple pleasure of combining the rice and meat sauce in its cooking vessel. Whisk the eggs in a small bowl with the milk and two-thirds of the grated parmesan. Add to the rice and meat mixture and combine well. Top with the remaining parmesan, then the breadcrumbs. Drizzle with the remaining oil. Bake the rice on the top rack of the oven for about 20 minutes, or until a crust develops. The goal is to finish the cooking of the rice, but allow it to retain some moisture from the sauce underneath the crust, so be careful not to overcook it.

STUFFAT TAL-FENEK

RABBIT STEW

PREPARATION: 30 MINUTES + MARINATING OVERNIGHT COOKING: 2 HOURS 10 MINUTES

This dish can be found in restaurants, homes and at most celebratory occasions. Rabbits were introduced by the Phoenicians, who arrived on the islands of Malta around 700 BCE. The animals soon became an important part of the local diet. The Maltese have a word for a rabbit feast – *fenkata* – and each year the traditional Mnarja festival features rabbit stew as the main dish.

It is critical to marinate the rabbit a day in advance to ensure the most tender and tasty result. The main flavours of the stew are bay and wine, so it is best to use fresh bay leaves and quality wine. A touch of sweetness pairs well with the meat, and some families add a splash of Malta's iconic soft drink, Kinnie, to the braise. This drink tastes somewhere between cola and chinotto, so I use the latter as a substitute. It is customary to serve the sauce with pasta as an entree, or the next day with leftover sauce.

INGREDIENTS

1 rabbit weighing about 1.5 kg
 (3 lb 5 oz), including the liver
 and kidneys
600 ml (20½ fl oz) red wine
5 garlic cloves, peeled
8 bay leaves
1 handful of any provincial herbs
 (such as thyme, rosemary or
 oregano) for marinating
salt and pepper
3 large ripe tomatoes or 400 g
 (14 oz) tinned diced tomatoes
2 tablespoons olive oil
2 onions, chopped
2 small carrots, finely grated
1 tablespoon tomato paste
 (concentrated purée)
100 ml (3½ fl oz) chinotto
5 medium potatoes,
 peeled and quartered
150 g (5½ oz) peas, rinsed if frozen

HOW TO

Cut the rabbit into small portions, and halve the liver. Marinate all the rabbit pieces overnight in the red wine, garlic cloves, half the bay leaves, the provincial herbs and some salt and pepper.

The following day, score the tomatoes on their bases (if using fresh) and grate with a box grater. Remove the rabbit pieces except liver and kidneys from the marinade (reserving the liquid) and pat dry with paper towel. Remove and discard the provincial herbs. In a heavy-based pot over a medium–high heat, fry the rabbit pieces in the oil in batches until browned all over. Return all the rabbit to the pot with the tomato, onion, carrot, tomato paste and remaining bay leaves. Add the marinade, liver, kidneys and chinotto. Bring to the boil over a high heat, then reduce the heat to low and simmer covered for about 2 hours. Add the potatoes in the last 30 minutes. Stir occasionally, adding water if the stew becomes dry.

Add the peas and cook for a few minutes more, then turn off the heat and let the stew sit for 15 minutes. You may wish to serve the traditional entree of sliced kidneys and sauce ladled on top of spaghetti. Serve the rabbit and vegetables with crusty bread and a salad.

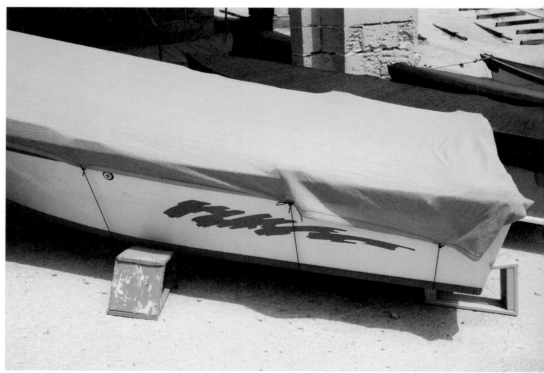

MAJJAL FIL-FORN

BRAISED PORK AND VEGETABLES

PREPARATION: 10 MINUTES COOKING: 1 HOUR 40 MINUTES

This is a simple dish that yields delicious results, similar to Maltese potatoes (page 185) with the addition of pork and zucchini (courgettes). Beef can also be used – but without the fennel and often with garlic instead. These recipes have their origins as dishes cooked gently in earthenware pots, over coal or beside the fire. The meat becomes tender and the vegetables are full of flavour. You can make this in a large ovenproof frying pan or a deep tray that can handle being placed on the stove.

INGREDIENTS

4–6 pork chops
 (800 g–1 kg/1 lb 12 oz–2 lb 3 oz)
salt and pepper
4 large potatoes, peeled and
 cut into 1 cm (½ in) slices
400 g (14 oz) zucchini (courgettes)
 or marrow (round zucchini), cut
 into 1.5 cm (½ in) slices
2 onions, thinly sliced
500 ml (17 fl oz/2 cups) chicken stock
1 tablespoon fennel seeds
chilli flakes (optional)
2 tablespoons olive oil

HOW TO

Place the pork chops in a large ovenproof frying pan or a flameproof deep tray. Season with salt and pepper. Layer the potatoes and zucchini evenly over the pork and scatter the onions on top, seasoning again. Pour in the stock and top up with water until the vegetables are almost covered. Sprinkle on the fennel seeds and chilli (if using) and drizzle the oil evenly over everything.

Cover with a lid or foil and bring to a simmer over a medium heat. Reduce the heat to low and cook for 1½ hours. Check the liquid level halfway through; it should reduce to a thick sauce, but if reducing too quickly, add a small splash of water.

Remove the lid or foil and place the pan under a hot grill (broiler) to crisp up the vegetables and onions. Serve with salad and bread.

BRAGIOLI
BEEF OLIVES

PREPARATION: 30 MINUTES COOKING: 1 HOUR 15 MINUTES

This Maltese staple does not actually contain olives. The word 'olive' in reference to sliced meat encasing a stuffing comes from the old French word '*alou*', meaning lark. The shape of the meat rolls was thought to resemble these birds without their heads.

For celebratory occasions, Maltese families are sure to grace the table with *bragioli*. Each household has its own version, with some using boiled eggs in the stuffing, and others braising the olives in tomato ragu or adding spice. My recipe honours the dish's fundamentals, using old bread and smoked pork, and peas to finish the sauce. Serve *bragioli* with boiled or mashed potatoes and a salad. The sauce is traditionally enjoyed over spaghetti as an entree.

BEEF OLIVES

250 g (9 oz) minced (ground) pork
250 g (9 oz) minced (ground) beef
100 g (3½ oz) smoked speck,
  diced (or use bacon)
1 onion, finely diced
2 garlic cloves, finely chopped
50 g (1¾ oz) fresh breadcrumbs,
  or torn bread without crusts from
  a continental-style loaf
50 g (1¾ oz) parmesan, grated
2 tablespoons chopped
  flat-leaf (Italian) parsley
salt and pepper
8 large thinly cut topside or round
  beef steaks (around 600 g/1 lb 5 oz)
1 tablespoon olive oil

SAUCE

1 onion, chopped
2 garlic cloves, finely chopped
1 medium carrot, grated
1 tablespoon olive oil
2 tablespoons tomato paste
  (concentrated purée)
250 ml (8½ fl oz/1 cup) red wine
  (a slightly sweet wine works well)
250 ml (8½ fl oz/1 cup) beef stock
2 bay leaves
salt and pepper
150 g (5½ oz) peas, rinsed if frozen

HOW TO

To make the stuffing, combine the minced meats, speck, onion, garlic, breadcrumbs, parmesan and parsley in a large bowl. Season well with salt and pepper and mix thoroughly.

Using a mallet or heavy glass bottle, pound the steaks between pieces of plastic wrap until 5 mm–1 cm (¼–½ in) thick. Thinner is better, but be careful not to tear the meat.

Take an eighth of the filling and place it in the middle of a flattened steak. Fold one end of the steak over the filling, tuck in the sides, and roll up. Secure with toothpicks or tie with kitchen string and place on a plate seam-side down. Continue to make rolls with the remaining steak and stuffing. Season the rolls on both sides.

Heat a heavy-based frying pan over a medium heat and add the oil and beef olives. Gently colour them on two sides, then transfer to a plate.

In the same pan, begin the sauce by sautéing the onion, garlic and carrot with the olive oil over a medium heat. Cook for 5 minutes without browning, then add the tomato paste, wine, stock, bay leaves, some salt and pepper and the beef olives. The liquid should come at least a third of the way up the beef (top up with water if needed). Place a lid or foil over the pan and simmer over a low heat for 1 hour. Turn the olives after 30 minutes and check the liquid level, adding water if necessary. Finish with the peas, cooking for a few minutes more. Remove from the heat and allow to sit for 10 minutes before serving.

SAUSAGE AND CAULIFLOWER WITH EGGS AND ĠBEJNIET

<u>PREPARATION</u>: 20 MINUTES <u>COOKING</u>: 1 HOUR 5 MINUTES

This is an easy bake inspired by a long agricultural chat over local delicacies on the island of Gozo. I love how the sausage flavours the vegetables, and how easily the eggs and fresh cheese complete the dish.

INGREDIENTS

3 large ripe tomatoes or 400 g
  (14 oz) tinned diced tomatoes
1 small onion, finely chopped
2 garlic cloves, finely sliced
1 teaspoon ground coriander
3 tablespoons extra-virgin olive oil
250 ml (8½ fl oz/1 cup) water
salt and pepper
1 small cauliflower (500–600 g/
  1 lb 2 oz–1 lb 5 oz), cut into florets
300 g (10½ oz) Italian pork
  sausages, cut into thirds
4 eggs
4 fresh Ġbejniet cheeselets
  (page 46) or 360 g (12½ oz)
  firm ricotta divided into 4 pieces
2 tablespoons chopped
  flat-leaf (Italian) parsley

HOW TO

If using fresh tomatoes, score them on their bases and grate with a box grater. Sauté the onion, garlic and coriander in 1 tablespoon of the oil until soft. Add the water and tomato and simmer for 10 minutes. Season with salt and pepper.

Preheat the oven to 190°C (375°F). Scoop the sauce into a deep medium-sized baking dish. Scatter the cauliflower and sausage over the sauce, season with salt and pepper and drizzle with another tablespoon of oil. Toss to coat the cauliflower and sausage in sauce. Cover well with foil and bake for 45 minutes, or until the cauliflower is soft through to the middle.

Make spaces for 4 eggs and crack them into the wells. Return to the oven uncovered for another few minutes, or until the eggs are cooked to your liking. Place a cheeselet or piece of ricotta in each corner of the dish and sprinkle the parsley all over. Drizzle with the remaining oil and plonk the dish in the middle of the table. Enjoy with a salad and crusty bread.

TIMPANA

SERVES 8

<u>PREPARATION</u>: 45 MINUTES + CHILLING <u>COOKING</u>: 2 HOURS 10 MINUTES

Timpana is one of Malta's most recognised dishes (known as '*timpano*' in Sicily). The pie is reserved for special occasions, though you would not think this given how often some Maltese people make it. The goal is to cook the pastry without drying the interior. To help with this, I make my *timpana* in a tall cake tin so the pie is high and not too wide. (If you don't have a tall tin, you can also make the pie in an enamelled cast-iron pot, skipping the crimped edge and serving the pie upside down.) Making and chilling the pasta filling in advance is another trick. The inclusion of minced pork adds moisture, and chicken livers add a distinctive flavour.

FILLING

3 large ripe tomatoes or 400 g (14 oz)
  tinned diced tomatoes
1 onion, finely diced
2 garlic cloves, finely chopped
1 tablespoon olive oil
400 g (14 oz) minced (ground) pork
100 g (3½ oz) pancetta or bacon,
  diced into 1 cm (½ in) pieces
2 tablespoons tomato paste
  (concentrated purée)
500 ml (17 fl oz/2 cups) chicken stock
½ teaspoon ground allspice
¼ teaspoon ground nutmeg
salt and pepper
180 g (6½ oz) chicken livers,
  membranes removed, diced into
  2 cm (¾ in) pieces
1½ tablespoons butter
300 g (10½ oz) macaroni
  (straight, not elbow) or penne
5 eggs (2 of them hard-boiled,
  peeled and quartered)
80 g (2¾ oz) parmesan, grated

SHORTCRUST PASTRY

450 g (1 lb/3 cups) plain
  (all-purpose) flour, plus extra
  for dusting
210 g (7½ oz) butter, chilled and
  diced, plus extra for greasing
½ teaspoon salt
100–120 ml (3½–4 fl oz) iced water

1 egg
2 tablespoons milk

HOW TO

If using fresh tomatoes, score them on their bases and grate with a box grater. Sauté the onion and garlic in the oil in a saucepan over a medium heat for 5 minutes. Add the minced meat and pancetta and cook until the meat has browned and any moisture has evaporated. Add the tomatoes, tomato paste, stock, spices and some salt and pepper and bring to the boil. Cover with a lid and simmer the ragu for 45 minutes. Scrape into a bowl to cool.

In a frying pan, sauté the liver in the butter over a medium heat until the pieces are seared all over but still pink in the middle. Season with salt and pepper.

Boil the pasta in well-salted water for a few minutes less than the packet recommends. Drain and rinse with cold water to cool the pasta down.

Whisk 3 eggs in a large mixing bowl, then stir in the parmesan. Mix in the pasta, followed by the ragu and chicken livers. The pasta should not be as wet as a normal pasta with sauce, but should not be too dry either. Refrigerate until completely chilled.

While the pasta mixture is chilling, make the pastry. Combine the

flour, butter and salt in a bowl and rub together with your fingertips until the mixture resembles breadcrumbs or rough sand. Add the water to create a firm dough. Shape into a ball, then flatten into a disc. Cover in plastic wrap and chill in the refrigerator for 45 minutes.

Preheat the oven to 180°C (360°F) and butter a large, tall non-stick springform cake tin (about 10 cm/4 in high and 24 cm/9½ in wide). Roll out the pastry on a floured surface to 5 mm (¼ in) thick. Line the tin with the pastry, then trim off the excess and form the scraps into a ball to use for the lid. Fill the pastry shell with half the pasta mixture. Scatter with the wedges of boiled egg, and top with the remaining pasta. Roll out the remaining pastry and cover the pie. Trim off the excess pastry leaving a small border. Fold in and use a thumb to make decorative indentations around the edge.

Whisk the egg with the milk and brush over the top of the *timpana*. Bake in the oven for 45 minutes, then run a knife around the edge of the pie, remove the springform sides and cook for another 15 minutes.

VEGETABLES

The stalls and vegetable vans are social magnets of sorts, existing as places to congregate and chat as well as buy quality produce.

The archipelago of Malta is rocky with limestone, but such is the appetite for homegrown vegetables that anywhere where space allows, there are plots of soil. Most produce is consumed by the growers, but also shared with family and neighbours or sold at roadside stalls. The stalls and vegetable vans are social magnets of sorts, existing as places to congregate and chat as well as buy produce.

The intensely seasonal vegetables are displayed in turquoise-coloured crates, signalling very fine produce to be found. The variety of vegetables grown on Malta includes tomatoes, zucchini (courgettes), broad beans, eggplant (aubergine), pumpkin (winter squash), cabbage and kohlrabi to name a few! Local potatoes are a feature of Gozitan cuisine. The dry soil actually produces a very tasty potato, exported in large quantities to northern countries in spring.

Vegetables are not only consumed as side dishes in Malta, and are often as significant as meat in dishes like stuffed vegetables or hearty stews where meat takes a back seat. Up until the last two centuries, the Maltese diet seldom featured meat, which was considered a luxury.

Perhaps this is why quality vegetables are highly regarded by the Maltese. It's a pleasure to see buyers peruse vendors' stalls finding the best produce. Reliance on vegetables grown close to home is critical for our future and considering the world's frightening over production of meat, you could argue that Malta is in a good place. Overtoiling the soil also has its negatives so it's exciting to see sustainable farming techniques popping up in Malta. These include circular farming, aquaponics and no-till farming (a method that decreases the amount of soil erosion). The future's looking good for Malta and its vegetables.

In the spirit of Maltese produce, I suggest using market-bought organic vegetables for the best results in the recipes ahead.

TOMATO, CAPER AND *ĠBEJNIET* SALAD

PREPARATION: 10 MINUTES COOKING: 3 MINUTES

I just can't kick the combination of tomatoes and capers – sweetness countered by that distinct salty, acidic punch. Add to that some creamy *ġbejniet* and you've got a side salad that marries the flavours of Malta. It's also very easy to whip up, so you're bound to make friends with it.

Frying the capers gives some texture and concentrates their flavour (but is not strictly necessary). For anyone wanting their salad with less dairy, a little grated semi-dried *ġbejniet* or ricotta salata can be used instead of the fresh cheese.

INGREDIENTS

50 g (1¾ oz/⅓ cup) capers,
 rinsed and patted dry
2 tablespoons of olive oil or vegetable
 oil for frying capers
3 tabespoons extra-virgin olive oil
 for serving
4 fresh *Ġbejniet* cheeselets
 (page 46) or 360 g (12½ oz)
 firm ricotta
600 g (1 lb 5 oz) ripe tomatoes
 (beefsteak are ideal), thickly sliced
½ red onion, finely sliced
salt and pepper
2 teaspoons red-wine or
 sherry vinegar
1 small handful mint leaves,
 roughly chopped
1 small handful basil leaves

HOW TO

In a saucepan, heat the capers in half the oil until they begin to fry, then become crispy. Scoop onto paper towel to drain.

Quarter the cheeselets, or break the ricotta into large pieces. Arrange the tomato slices and pieces of cheese on a large platter and scatter with the onion. Sprinkle with salt and pepper, then drizzle with the remaining oil and vinegar. Top with the capers and herbs. Serve with crusty bread.

QAQOĊĊ MIMLI

STUFFED ARTICHOKES

PREPARATION: 30 MINUTES + 30 MINUTES SOAKING COOKING: 1 HOUR 10 MINUTES

Artichokes grow all over the islands of Malta, native to the Mediterranean and at home in the dry climate. This dish is a Maltese classic, designed for sharing as an appetiser. You eat the artichokes with your fingers, plucking each petal and scraping your teeth along them, rewarded with stuffing and a little flesh. When you reach the fibrous choke below the petals, simply scoop it out, then continue to eat the artichoke heart with teaspoons.

Some Maltese cooks stuff their artichokes with tuna; others include capers. Really you can use any mixture you like, but in my opinion anchovies and garlic are mandatory. When buying artichokes, look for those with prickly tips at the ends of their petals, as this means they are very fresh.

INGREDIENTS

2 large artichokes
  (or 4 smaller artichokes)
½ lemon, zested and juiced
5 anchovy fillets, finely chopped
100 g (3½ oz/1 cup) dry
  breadcrumbs
2 tablespoons black olives,
  pitted and finely chopped
2 tablespoons chopped
  flat-leaf (Italian) parsley
1 tablespoon chopped mint
2 garlic cloves, crushed
2 tablespoons olive oil,
  plus extra to drizzle
salt and pepper
2 medium potatoes, peeled
  and halved
100 ml (3½ fl oz) white vinegar

HOW TO

To prepare the artichokes, start by cutting off the stalks but don't throw them away. Soak the heads in a bowl of water with the lemon juice added for 30 minutes.

Meanwhile, prepare the stuffing. Deeply peel the skin from the artichoke stalks (it is fibrous and bitter), then dice the inner stalks as finely as you can. Combine in a bowl with the lemon zest and remaining ingredients except the potatoes and vinegar. Season with some salt and pepper and mix well.

Remove the artichoke heads from the water and place upside down on a hard surface. Smash each one to loosen and open up the petals. Turn the artichokes over and use scissors to cut off any sharp tips on the petals. Use your hands to spread the petals back further to make enough room to stuff in between. Start putting stuffing into all the gaps, using a teaspoon to get it deep down.

Place the potatoes and stuffed artichokes in the bottom of a saucepan. The potatoes are included to help to keep the artichokes upright, so choose a pan that fits them all snugly. Pour the vinegar into the base of the pan and add water to one-third of the way up the vegetables. Season with salt. Cover with a lid and simmer for 1 hour or longer (topping up with water as it evaporates), until the artichoke petals pluck out easily.

Heat the grill (broiler) of your oven and transfer the artichokes to a heatproof pan or dish. Drizzle them with extra oil and grill just until the breadcrumb stuffing begins to brown on top and is no longer wet. Serve the artichokes and potatoes with crusty bread.

EGGPLANT, MINT AND PEPPERED *ĠBEJNIET*

PREPARATION: 15 MINUTES + 20 MINUTES SOAKING COOKING: 25 MINUTES

In this recipe, the peppery and salty flavour of the semi-dried cheese counters the sweet and sour of the dressing. Soaking the eggplants in milk removes some of their bitterness and makes them really creamy when roasted. Serve as a side dish, or with crusty bread as a light meal.

INGREDIENTS

600–800 g (1 lb 5 oz–1 lb 12 oz)
  eggplants (aubergines), cut
  lengthways into eighths
500 ml (17 fl oz/2 cups) milk
salt and pepper
2 tablespoons extra-virgin olive oil
2 tablespoons honey
1 tablespoon red-wine
  or sherry vinegar
2 tablespoons chopped chives
2 tablespoons pine nuts
1 semi-dried peppered *ġbejniet*
  cheeselet (pages 46–47), or
  substitute 50 g (1¾ oz) ricotta
  salata with some freshly ground
  black pepper
1 handful mint leaves, torn

HOW TO

Combine the eggplant wedges and milk in a dish that fits the eggplant snugly, and leave to soak for 20 minutes. If the eggplant is not completely submerged, turn the wedges after 10 minutes.

Preheat the oven to 200°C (400°F). Drain and pat the eggplant dry. Spread on a baking tray and season with salt and pepper. Drizzle with 1 tablespoon of the oil and toss until the eggplant is evenly coated. Roast in the oven for 25 minutes, until soft in the middle and golden on the outside.

Meanwhile, mix the honey, vinegar, chives and remaining oil in a large bowl. As soon as the eggplant comes out of the oven, toss briefly with the sweet and sour dressing, then remove the pieces to a large platter and leave to cool to room temperature.

Toast the pine nuts in a dry frying pan over a low heat until golden, keeping a close eye on them as they burn easily.

Grate the cheese on the large holes of a grater. Scatter it over the eggplant, along with the mint and pine nuts. Drizzle over any remaining dressing.

SAUTÉED GREENS WITH ANCHOVIES AND LEMON

PREPARATION: 15 MINUTES COOKING: 5 MINUTES

With all the pasta, pastry and tomato-based dishes found in Maltese cuisine, any recipe heavy on the greens is welcome. I like to serve this with dishes such as *Timpana* (page 161) or Braised pork and vegetables (page 155).

INGREDIENTS

600 g (1 lb 5 oz) English spinach
3 tablespoons extra-virgin olive oil
1 garlic clove, finely chopped
6 anchovy fillets, finely chopped,
  plus 1 tablespoon oil from the jar
⅛ teaspoon chilli flakes (optional)
grated zest of ½ lemon
1 semi-dried *ġbejniet* (page 46–47)
  or 50 g (1¾ oz) ricotta salata, grated

HOW TO

Cut the roots from the spinach and wash and drain the leaves. Remove the excess water by tipping the leaves onto a clean tea towel (dish towel) and patting dry.

Heat 2 tablespoons of the oil in a large frying pan over a low heat and add the garlic, anchovies and their oil, and chilli if desired. Sauté until the anchovies break right down and the garlic is fragrant.

Add the spinach and lemon zest and increase the heat to medium. Cook for around 2 minutes, tossing, until wilted.

Serve on a plate topped with the grated cheese and drizzled with the remaining oil. This salad can also be served chilled.

KAPUNATA

PREPARATION: 20 MINUTES COOKING: 50 MINUTES

We all know about ratatouille since it became a movie hit. Well, *kapunata* (or *'caponata'* as it is known in Sicily) is its vibrant cousin from the south. *Kapunata* differs from ratatouille in that it balances sweet with sour and includes capers, olives, raisins and pine nuts. To limit the time spent frying batches of vegetables in pans, I roast some of my vegetables; it simplifies the process but also concentrates the flavour.

    Kapunata makes a great side to roasted meats, but I love to take inspiration from south of Malta in North Africa, adding eggs to make the dish like *shakshouka*.

INGREDIENTS

1 red capsicum (bell pepper)
1 eggplant (aubergine)
2 tablespoons olive oil
salt and pepper
4 medium-sized ripe tomatoes
4 garlic cloves
2 tablespoons pine nuts
1 onion, finely diced
2 celery stalks, finely diced
2 teaspoons sugar
100 ml (3½ fl oz) water
2 tablespoons capers, rinsed
2 tablespoons black olives,
 pitted and chopped
1 tablespoon raisins, chopped
2 teaspoons red-wine vinegar
1 tablespoon chopped mint
2 tablespoons chopped basil

HOW TO

Preheat the oven to 220°C (430°F). Cut the capsicum in half and remove the seeds. Slice the top off the eggplant, then cut it into quarters lengthways. Combine the capsicum and eggplant on a baking tray. Rub with 1 tablespoon of the oil and season with salt and pepper. Roast for 15 minutes.

Cut the cores out of the tomatoes. Reduce the oven heat to 200°C (400°F) and add the tomatoes and whole garlic cloves to the tray. Roast for another 20 minutes.

Meanwhile, lightly toast the pine nuts in a dry frying pan. Remove to a bowl and add the remaining oil, onion and celery to the pan. Sauté over a medium heat until soft (around 8 minutes). Season with salt and pepper. Add the toasted pine nuts and toss through briefly, then remove from the heat.

When the roasted vegetables are cool enough to handle, cut the capsicum into 1 cm (½ in) slices. Cut the eggplant into 2 cm (¾ in) pieces, and quarter the tomatoes. Add the roasted vegetables to the pan of onion and celery and return to the heat. Squeeze the garlic cloves from their skins into the pan. Add the sugar and water and simmer for 5 minutes, allowing the tomato to break up. Add the capers, olives, raisins and vinegar. Check the seasoning, then remove from the heat. Stir through the mint and basil. Serve warm or cold.

KAPUNATA SHAKSHOUKA
Preheat the oven to 200°C (400°F). Scoop the kapunata into an ovenproof dish (or individual dishes) and stir through a splash of water to loosen up the sauce. Create wells in the sauce and crack an egg into each. Bake uncovered until the eggs are cooked to your liking. Serve with crusty bread.

Genuine, friendly, resilient.
Spirited, nosy! A good kind of loud.
Hospitable and generous - family comes first, but friends too.
When the barrier breaks, consider yourself one of them.
A complex past.
Progressive today.
These are the people of Malta.

MINESTRA TAL-ḪAXIX

VEGETABLE SOUP

PREPARATION: 20 MINUTES + OVERNIGHT SOAKING COOKING: 1 HOUR 5 MINUTES

With recipes passed from generation to generation, *minestra* has been around for as long as anyone can remember. Discussions take place between and within families about which vegetables should be used. Another point of contention is whether the soup should be mashed or kept chunky. I prefer the latter. Yes, *minestra* is similar to Italian minestrone, however *minestra* has its differences: pumpkin adds some sweetness, the vegetables are in large pieces (or mashed) and the common legume included is *favetta* (split fava beans). Maltese *kusksu* pasta is sometimes added. Despite the warm climate in Malta, this soup is enjoyed year round and a pot of it is often found in the fridge of Maltese homes.

INGREDIENTS

100 g (3½ oz) split broad (fava)
  beans, soaked overnight
1 large onion, finely diced
2 small carrots, diced into 3 cm
  (1¼ in) pieces
1 celery stalk including leaves,
  finely diced
1 tablespoon extra-virgin olive oil,
  plus extra to serve
1 bay leaf
1 leek, finely sliced
½ small white cabbage, thickly sliced
1 tablespoon tomato paste
  (concentrated purée)
1 teaspoon salt
200 g (7 oz) pumpkin (winter squash),
  peeled, seeded and cut in large
  chunks
3 small potatoes, peeled and
  quartered
1 medium zucchini (courgette),
  cut in 6 cm (2½ in) chunks
1 large handful flat-leaf
  (Italian) parsley, chopped
shaved parmesan, to serve

HOW TO

Drain and rinse the soaked beans. In a large saucepan, sauté the onion, carrot and celery in the oil over a low–medium heat for 5 minutes, stirring often. Stir in the beans, bay leaf, leek, cabbage, tomato paste and salt. Cover with water and simmer for 20 minutes with the lid on. Add the pumpkin and potato and cook for another 20 minutes, then add the zucchini and cook for 20 minutes more. If the soup becomes too thick during cooking, add more water, and also taste for seasoning.

Stir through most of the parsley, saving a little for garnish. Ladle into bowls and top with a drizzle of oil, shavings of parmesan, and parsley. Serve with crusty bread.

SOPPA TAL-ARMLA
WIDOW'S SOUP

PREPARATION: 20 MINUTES COOKING: 45 MINUTES

This soup is said to have acquired its name due to the ease with which its simple ingredients could be found; even a widow of basic or little means could procure them. As a broad rule, only white and green vegetables are included. I like to make the soup without tomato paste as I think the flavour of the vegetables comes through better, especially when you use a nice homemade vegetable stock. The addition of *ġbejniet* cheese and eggs turn the soup into a sustaining meal.

INGREDIENTS

1 large onion, finely chopped

1 garlic clove, finely chopped

1 small kohlrabi (about
  300 g/10½ oz), peeled and diced
  into 2 cm (¾ in) pieces

1 large celery stalk, finely diced

1 tablespoon extra-virgin olive oil,
  plus extra to serve

1 tablespoon tomato paste
  (concentrated purée), optional

½ medium cauliflower, cut into
  small florets

500 g (1 lb 2 oz) potatoes, peeled
  and diced into 3 cm (1¼ in) pieces

2 bay leaves

1 litre (34 fl oz/4 cups)
  vegetable stock

150 g (5½ oz) podded broad (fava)
  beans, or you can use peas

1 medium zucchini (courgette),
  cut into 4 cm (1½ in) chunks

salt and pepper

4 eggs

4 fresh Ġbejniet cheeselets
  (page 46) or 360 g (12½ oz)
  firm ricotta divided into 4 pieces

roughly chopped flat-leaf (Italian)
  parsley, to serve

HOW TO

In a large saucepan, sauté the onion, garlic, kohlrabi and celery in the oil over a low–medium heat for 8 minutes, stirring often. Stir in the tomato paste (if using), then add the cauliflower, potatoes, bay leaves and stock. Top up with water if necessary to cover the vegetables. Simmer with a lid on for about 20 minutes, until the vegetables are tender. Now add the broad beans and zucchini and season with salt and pepper. Cook for another 10 minutes.

Crack the eggs into the top of the soup to poach. Cook with the lid on for a few minutes.

Ladle the soup into 4 bowls with an egg in each one. Add a cheeselet (or piece of ricotta) to each bowl, to melt and crumble into the soup. Scatter with the parsley and drizzle with extra-virgin olive oil. Serve with crusty bread.

PATATA FIL-FORN
MALTESE POTATOES

PREPARATION: 15 MINUTES COOKING: 1 HOUR

This popular dish is the perfect accompaniment to many meat and seafood dishes found in this book. It's a feat of simple engineering – the stock creates steam, which cooks up through the potatoes, keeping the bottom soft while the top develops a beautiful crust. These contrasting textures are delivered with the aromatics of fennel seed. Another bonus is the dish is so quick to prepare.

INGREDIENTS

800 g (1 lb 12 oz) potatoes,
  peeled and sliced 5 mm–1 cm
  (¼–½ in) thick
1 medium onion, thinly sliced
2 garlic cloves, thinly sliced
2 tablespoons chopped
  flat-leaf (Italian) parsley
1 tablespoon fennel seeds,
  plus more for the top if desired
2 tablespoons olive oil
salt
250 ml (8½ fl oz/1 cup)
  chicken stock

HOW TO

Preheat the oven to 180°C (360°F). Combine the potatoes, onion, garlic, parsley, fennel and 1 tablespoon of the oil in a medium baking dish. Season with salt and mix with your hands until all the potatoes are coated in oil. Flatten the top layer of potatoes, then pour on the stock. If you like fennel as much as I do, sprinkle a little more over the top to get browned and crunchy. Drizzle with the remaining oil and bake uncovered for 1 hour. Test the potatoes with a skewer or fork – they should be soft all the way through with a little blistering on top.

QARABAGĦLI MIMLI FIL-FORN
STUFFED MARROWS

PREPARATION: 25 MINUTES COOKING: 1 HOUR 10 MINUTES

Marrow is a distinctive vegetable in the zucchini (courgette) family that withstands dry soil and grows well all over Malta. The common variety is round and green, and it could well be the country's most popular vegetable, as every corner grocer sells them almost all year round. Marrow are very versatile: when new and tender, around the size of an egg, it's best to blanch them and dress with lemon juice and olive oil. Once the size of oranges, they are great in stews and soups, and when larger, they are perfect for stuffing.

The basic premise of this dish is to combine the vegetable's flesh with minced meat, stuff it back in the skin, and bake it in the oven. Variations on the filling are endless, but I love the combination of pork, chilli and fennel. To make a more substantial meal, these are often roasted on top of Maltese potatoes (page 185), omitting the sauce of this recipe. Look for marrows in Turkish grocers, or use regular zucchini cut in half to make boats (and bake for 10 minutes less).

SAUCE

1 tablespoon olive oil
1 onion, finely chopped
2 garlic cloves, finely chopped
1 bay leaf
2 tablespoons tomato paste
  (concentrated purée)
500 ml (17 fl oz/2 cups) vegetable
  or chicken stock

STUFFED MARROWS

1 tablespoon fennel seeds
1 pinch of chilli flakes (optional)
1 teaspoon salt
4 marrows (round zucchini/
  courgettes) weighing about
  300 g (10½ oz) each
1 egg
400 g (14 oz) minced (ground) pork
  (not too lean – some fat adds
  moisture)
2 tablespoons dry breadcrumbs,
  plus extra to sprinkle
40 g (1½ oz) parmesan, grated,
  plus extra to sprinkle

HOW TO

To make the sauce, heat the oil in a saucepan over a medium heat and add the onion, garlic and bay leaf. Sauté for 5 minutes, until the onion is soft and translucent. Add the tomato paste and stock and simmer for 15 minutes, then remove from the heat.

Toast the fennel seeds in a dry pan until fragrant, then grind with a mortar and pestle along with the chilli flakes (if using) and salt.

Slice off the top fifth of each marrow. Use a spoon to remove the interior flesh, leaving the shell a few centimetres (under an inch) thick. Finely chop the flesh of 2 of the marrows. You can discard the tops, but keep the leftover flesh for another recipe (e.g. throw it in a tomato sauce).

Preheat the oven to 200°C (400°F). Whisk the egg in a mixing bowl and add the chopped marrow, ground fennel, pork, breadcrumbs and parmesan. Stir well. Stuff each marrow with the mixture. Pour the tomato sauce into a deep baking dish (about 20 × 30 cm/ 8 × 12 in). Place the marrows on top of the sauce and sprinkle with extra breadcrumbs. Cover with foil and bake for 40 minutes. Remove the foil, sprinkle some extra parmesan on the marrows and cook for another 5–10 minutes to brown the tops. Serve with salad and crusty bread.

SWEETS & DRINKS

Religion exerts itself on baking year round, with a sweet treat never more than a saint's day away.

For a long time, Malta had access to spices and flavours that were hugely exotic on the mainland of continental Europe. There's no doubt of an Arabic influence in Maltese desserts. Dates are frequently used in sweet dishes, and there is even a local recipe for *halva* (page 211).

Religion exerts itself on baking year round, with a sweet treat never more than a saint's day away. Over ninety per cent of the population identifies as Catholic (Roman Catholicism is declared the state religion), forming the basis of many culinary traditions.

Christmas celebrates chestnuts. Like dates, these are not grown on Malta, but dried chestnuts feature in old recipes. They are rehydrated and some people use them in a pie, while many still make a thick drink of chestnuts, cocoa and spices known as *imbuljuta* (page 227).

Unlike dates and chestnuts, prickly pears and honey are harvested on Malta and occur frequently in desserts. Maltese honey is recognised for its unique flavourings through the seasons and prickly pears are used to make jams and liqueur, which you'll find hard to miss when passing through the airport's duty free store.

The *prinjolata*, a festive cake featuring pine nuts (page 228), is served in the lead up to Lent. Carob is another theme of Lent, appreciated for its taste and also considered to have healing properties. Carob beans come from a tree that is indigenous to the Mediterranean and found growing on Malta.

Ahead in this chapter are examples of classic Maltese sweets, plus some modern interpretations using the ingredients of the islands.

KWAREŻIMAL

LENTEN ALMOND BISCUITS

PREPARATION: 15 MINUTES COOKING: 25 MINUTES

Vegan by default, this recipe has no eggs or dairy because of its association with Lent. (The name comes from 'Quaresima', the Italian word for Lent. In Maltese, Lent is called 'Randan', which interestingly stems from the Arabic/Muslim 'Ramadan'.)

Some recipes include egg and even cocoa powder, but for authenticity and the practical reason that it's great to have a treat for vegan friends or family, I make my biscuits the original way. Traditionally, the size of the biscuits is unusually large – perhaps they were intended to be nibbled at over the Lent period. I prefer to slice them smaller once they are out of the oven, to make them more sharing friendly. If orange zest isn't your thing, lemon zest also works wonderfully. These are more-ish, but should you have leftovers, they can be stored in a container for up to two weeks.

INGREDIENTS

200 g (7 oz/2 cups) ground almonds
200 g (7 oz/1⅓ cups) plain
 (all-purpose) flour
200 g (7 oz) sugar
1 teaspoon baking powder
1 teaspoon ground cinnamon
grated zest of ½ large orange
125 ml (4 fl oz/½ cup) water
2 tablespoons honey
50 g (1¾ oz/⅓ cup) almonds,
 toasted and chopped

HOW TO

Combine the ground almonds, flour, sugar, baking powder, cinnamon and zest in a food processor and process for 20 seconds. Gradually add the water about a tablespoon at a time until the mixture darkens in colour and forms a dough that is slightly dry and crumbly (you may not need all the water). Spill the contents onto a work surface and form into a ball. If you find it is too dry to come together, return it to the mixer and process with some more water.

Preheat the oven to 180°C (360°F) and line a baking tray with baking paper. Divide the dough into 4 balls. Flatten these into rectangular shapes and roll out to approximately 15 cm (6 in) long, 5 cm (2 in) wide and 2 cm (¾ in) thick. Transfer to the tray and bake for 20–25 minutes. The edges should brown, and you should be able to lift up each biscuit with a spatula.

Working quickly while the biscuits are hot, brush them with the honey and sprinkle over the chopped almonds, then cut each bar on a slight angle into 5–6 smaller pieces. Allow to cool.

QAGĦAQ TAL-GĦASEL

HONEY RINGS

<u>PREPARATION</u>: 30 MINUTES <u>COOKING</u>: 25 MINUTES

These unique rings of pastry are called honey rings because they were once made with a byproduct of honey – honeycomb melted down after the honey was extracted. Today the filling is always made with treacle.

<u>PASTRY</u>

400 g (14 oz/2⅔ cups)
  plain (all-purpose) flour
100 g (3½ oz) fine semolina
150 g (5½ oz) butter, chilled
  and diced
1 egg yolk
150 ml (5 fl oz) strained orange juice,
  or water

<u>FILLING</u>

400 g (14 oz) dark treacle
  or molasses
100 g (3½ oz) dark chocolate,
  broken into chunks
grated zest of ½ lemon
grated zest of ½ orange
1 teaspoon mixed (pumpkin pie) spice
1 teaspoon ground cinnamon
1 teaspoon ground aniseed
200 ml (7 fl oz) water
150 g (5½ oz) fine semolina,
  plus extra for dusting

<u>HOW TO</u>

To make the pastry, combine the flour, semolina and butter in a bowl and rub together with your fingertips until the mixture resembles breadcrumbs or rough sand. Mix in the egg yolk and half the juice or water to form a dough. Keep adding liquid until the dough is no longer dry. Cover the dough and set aside to rest while you make the filling.

Combine the filling ingredients except the semolina in a saucepan and bring to a simmer over a medium heat, stirring until the chocolate has melted. Whisk in the semolina and cook over a low heat for 4 minutes. Remove from the heat and set aside to cool into a malleable paste. If too wet, continue cooking or add more semolina.

Line 2 baking trays with baking paper. Dust a work surface with a little extra semolina and shape the pastry into a log. Roll out to a long rectangle, 100 cm (40 in) long and 16 cm (6¼ in) wide. Cut the rectangle at 10 cm (4 in) intervals to form strips. Form a line of filling lengthways down the middle of each pastry strip, stopping just short of the ends. Roll the pastry around the filling to enclose. Bend one end of the pastry around to meet the other, creating a ring. Pinch the ends together and place on a tray. Continue making rings with the remaining strips.

Preheat the oven to 180°C (360°F). Use a small sharp-tipped knife to make 6 angular slits around the top of each ring. Bake in the oven for 15–20 minutes, or until golden but not browned. Allow to cool before serving. The rings will keep in a sealed container for up to 3 weeks if kept in a dry, cool environment.

BISKUTTINI TAL-LEWZ

ALMOND MACAROONS

PREPARATION: 10 MINUTES COOKING: 15 MINUTES

The perfect macaroon should be crisp on the outside and chewy in the middle. These keep well and are perfect for family occasions, ideal for serving with coffee. I like to flavour mine with a touch of orange-blossom water (*ilma żahar*) instead of the traditional almond essence.

Making *ilma żahar* in Malta is a fading craft, often made in monasteries by nuns, but still carried out by people such as Lawrence Bajada in Xagħra on the island of Gozo. In spring the flowers and leaves of the orange tree are gathered then steamed for hours. Droplets of condensation slowly collect to become the blossom water (*ilma żahar*), which is said to have medicinal benefits, being good for anxiety, aiding digestion, and even used for sick animals in the old days. Many old Maltese sweets recipes call for it but nowadays orange zest is more commonly used.

INGREDIENTS

200 g (7 oz) caster (superfine) sugar
2 large egg whites
½ teaspoon orange-blossom water
200 g (7 oz/2 cups) ground almonds
45 g (1½ oz/¼ cup) rice flour
blanched almonds

HOW TO

Preheat the oven to 170°C (340°F) and line a baking tray with baking paper. Whisk the sugar and egg whites together until the mixture becomes glossy and smooth. Mix in the orange-blossom water, then fold in the almonds and rice flour. Scoop up a heaped teaspoon of mixture and use a second spoon to scrape it onto the tray. Continue dolloping macaroons until you have used all the mixture. Press a blanched almond on top of each one. Bake for 15 minutes if you like them soft, or a little longer if you prefer them crunchier.

BAY LEAF
PANNA COTTA
AND MULBERRIES

PREPARATION: 5 MINUTES + 35 MINUTES RESTING COOKING: 20 MINUTES

These three ingredients grow on Malta, but don't get used as often as they could. This dessert showcases them in an easy recipe that I keep coming back to. Dried mulberries and carob syrup are available at health-food stores.

INGREDIENTS

400 ml (13½ fl oz) pouring cream
 (single/light)
100 ml (3½ fl oz) milk
80 g (2¾ oz) white chocolate,
 broken into pieces
5 dried bay leaves
1½ teaspoons powdered gelatine
1½ tablespoons water

DRUNK MULBERRIES

3 tablespoons carob syrup
60 ml (2 fl oz/¼ cup) water
100 g (3½ oz) dried mulberries

HOW TO

Gently heat the cream, milk and chocolate in a saucepan. Allow the chocolate to melt and the mixture to steam but not simmer.

Meanwhile, heat a dry frying pan over a medium heat and lightly toast the bay leaves on both sides until fragrant. Add them to the hot milk mixture. Keep the mixture on a very low heat just below simmering for 15 minutes (use a simmer mat if needed). Remove from the heat.

Sprinkle the gelatine into the water in a small bowl and leave to bloom for 5 minutes. Whisk into the saucepan of cream. Let the mixture sit for 30 minutes,

whisking at least 3 times. Strain through a fine sieve into a jug, then pour into 4 small bowls or glasses. Cover the panna cottas with plastic wrap and chill in the refrigerator for 4 hours, or until set.

While the panna cottas are setting, combine the carob syrup and water in a saucepan and bring to a simmer. Put the mulberries in a bowl and pour the hot syrup over the top. Stir the mulberries, then cover and leave to soak for at least 1 hour.

To serve, spoon some carob mulberries over each panna cotta.

SHEEP'S MILK AND STRAWBERRY PARFAIT WITH PISTACHIO NUTS

PREPARATION: 20 MINUTES + 8 HOURS FREEZING COOKING: 15 MINUTES

The best ice cream I have ever eaten was made of sheep's milk and strawberries from the Tal-Karmnu farm outside Valletta (the capital of Malta). The local strawberries overwhelmed me through the creaminess, and just like that, on a stone wall under the pelting heat, I realised I had eaten 500 ml of ice cream. I have developed this recipe – an ode to their magnificent product – as a parfait, because not everyone owns an ice cream maker.

INGREDIENTS

4 eggs, separated
165 g (6 oz/¾ cup) sugar
750 ml (25½ fl oz/3 cups)
  sheep's milk (or cow's)
1 teaspoon natural vanilla extract
250 g (9 oz) strawberries
200 ml (7 fl oz) pouring cream

TO SERVE

2 tablespoons chopped
  pistachio nuts
250 g (9 oz) strawberries
1 tablespoon honey

HOW TO

Whisk the egg yolks with ½ cup of the sugar in a medium saucepan, then whisk in the milk. Place over a medium heat and stir almost constantly. Allow the mixture to heat and then thicken to a light custard (you should be able to draw a line through the custard on the back of a spoon without it running). Strain the custard through a fine sieve into a large bowl. Whisk in the vanilla and set aside to cool to room temperature.

While the custard is cooling, cut the strawberries into a fine dice and whip the cream.

Beat the egg whites to soft peaks in a medium bowl. Gradually rain in the remaining sugar and beat to stiff peaks. Fold the whipped cream through the cooled custard, followed by the egg whites. Now fold in the diced strawberries. Line a loaf (bar) tin approximately 30 × 15 cm (12 × 6 in) with plastic wrap, and pour in the mixture. Freeze for at least 8 hours or overnight.

Lightly toast the pistachio nuts in a dry frying pan. Cut the extra strawberries in half and place in a bowl. Drizzle with the honey and stir gently. Cut the parfait into slices and serve with the strawberries and a sprinkle of pistachio nuts.

PUDINA TAL-ĦOBŻ

BREAD PUDDING

PREPARATION: 15 MINUTES + 1 HOUR SOAKING COOKING: 30 MINUTES

Don't throw away your old bread! *Pudina tal-ħobż* is a beloved recipe passed down through the generations. No two families make it the same, but commonly sugar, butter, eggs and cocoa are added to soaked bread. Grated citrus zest, dried fruits and spices all help to give the hearty pudding some gusto. The result is not the most attractive of desserts, but it's delicious and easy to make. I like to serve it just warm with whipped cream. It can also be eaten cold cut in slices, a perfect sweet snack on the go.

INGREDIENTS

600 g (1 lb 5 oz) continental-style
  white loaf, unsliced
500 ml (17 fl oz/2 cups) milk
50 g (1¾ oz) butter, plus extra
  for greasing
130 g (4½ oz) sugar
3 eggs
2 tablespoons unsweetened
  cocoa powder
1 teaspoon baking powder
grated zest of 1 orange
1 teaspoon mixed spice
½ teaspoon natural vanilla extract
50 g (1¾ oz) dates, pitted and
  chopped, or sultanas
splash of brandy or sherry (optional)

HOW TO

Cut the crust from the loaf of bread, then slice around 5 cm (2 in) thick. Cut or tear into 5 cm (2 in) pieces. Place in a bowl and cover with the milk. Press down on the bread then leave to soak for 1 hour.

Cream the butter and sugar in a large mixing bowl until pale. Whisk in the eggs, cocoa and baking powder, then stir in the remaining ingredients. Add the soaked bread (leaving any milk in the bowl behind) and stir until evenly combined. There shouldn't be any dry patches of bread – if there is, add some of the milk.

Preheat the oven to 180°C (360°F) and butter a large cake tin or baking dish of any shape. Tip the bread mixture into the dish and press down on the mixture firmly so there are no loose pockets. Bake for about 30 minutes, until just cooked through (test by inserting a skewer in the centre of the pudding – it should come out clean).

MALTESE COFFEE GRANITA AND WHIPPED RICOTTA

PREPARATION: 20 MINUTES + 4 HOURS FREEZING COOKING: 10 MINUTES

Traditional Maltese coffee is a heady brew containing spices and chicory that is still appreciated today, particularly by the older generation. Chicory is a plant like dandelion. When its root is roasted and ground, it shares some attributes with coffee while being great for digestion (you can find it at health-food shops). Some suggest the inclusion of chicory and spices in Maltese coffee came about during times when coffee was scarce and the quality inferior. This granita is one of my favourite ices, as the spices give the coffee a lift and the egg whites soften the ice crystals, helping the texture. Paired with sweet ricotta cream, the dessert somehow has a whiff of tiramisu about it.

INGREDIENTS

500 ml (17 fl oz/2 cups) water
30 g (1 oz) freshly ground
  coffee beans
2 teaspoons roasted ground
  chicory root
100 g (3½ oz) sugar
½ teaspoon ground cloves
½ teaspoon ground aniseed
2 egg whites

WHIPPED RICOTTA

400 g (14 oz) ricotta
grated zest of ½ lemon
1½ tablespoons honey
1 tablespoon milk

HOW TO

Heat the water with the coffee, chicory, sugar and spices until just simmering. Turn the heat to very low and keep the mixture below simmering for 7 minutes (use a simmer mat if needed). Pour through a paper coffee filter or 3 layers of muslin (cheesecloth) into a bowl. Allow to cool.

Whisk the egg whites in a separate mixing bowl until foamy. Whisk in the coffee mixture, then pour into a wide glass or ceramic dish. Freeze for 1 hour.

Use a fork to scrape the ice crystals from the edges of the dish and blend them into the unfrozen centre. Return to the freezer and repeat every 30–40 minutes, until the mixture has become ice crystals throughout. You should rake the ice crystals 3 or 4 times.

Meanwhile, put the ricotta in a mixing bowl and break it up with a whisk. Add the zest, honey and milk and whisk together until you have a smooth but firm consistency similar to cake frosting (you may need a little more milk).

To serve, scoop some ricotta mixture onto plates or bowls and make wells in the centre with the back of the spoon. Scoop coffee granita into the wells.

HELWA TAT-TORK

HALVA

PREPARATION: 5 MINUTES COOKING: 10-15 MINUTES

The Maltese name for *halva* translates to 'Turk's sweet'. Found in many Middle Eastern countries, *halva* is loved in Malta too. I'm curious as to why tahini hasn't made its way into savoury recipes, as it's readily available, but regardless, the sweet is here to stay. The tahini confection is commonly made with almonds, but since discovering that some pecan trees grow on Malta, I've been using those instead with great results. They toast lightly under the molten heat of the halva, and are less dense than almonds. I love this halva's citrus flavour with both orange-blossom water and zest. If you are not a fan of this flavour, this recipe might just convert you!

INGREDIENTS

260 g (9 oz) light (hulled) tahini
1 teaspoon natural vanilla extract
1 teaspoon orange-blossom water
grated zest of 1 orange
80 g (2¾ oz) pecans
200 g (7 oz) sugar
180 ml (6 fl oz) water

HOW TO

Line a small loaf (bar) tin with baking paper. Warm the tahini in a medium saucepan over the lowest heat until tepid, then stir in the vanilla, orange-blossom water, orange zest and pecans and remove from the heat.

Meanwhile, heat the sugar and water in a small saucepan over a low heat. The sugar will dissolve, then the syrup will come to the boil (resist stirring once it starts simmering). Cook until it reaches 140°C (285°F) on a sugar thermometer. The syrup should remain clear without any caramelising, and there should be so many bubbles you can no longer see liquid.

As soon as the sugar is cooked, pour it into the warm tahini mixture and stir quickly until blended, then immediately scrape into the tin. Before long it will harden into a grainy confection. Leave to cool for at least 1 hour.

Cut the *halva* into small squares. *Halva* can be stored for weeks in an airtight container.

SINIZZA

PREPARATION: 40 MINUTES COOKING: 45 MINUTES

Malta's indulgent take on a Swiss roll has all the bells and whistles. An outer layer of pastry envelops sponge cake with a sweet ricotta filling, which can be flavoured at will. I love to include dark chocolate, and use Prickly pear liqueur (page 217) for sprinkling onto the cake. Other recipes include orange-blossom water, nutmeg or glacé cherries. This is a fun project that yields a rich, memorable dessert reminiscent of cannoli (or 'kannoli' in Malta). Just don't count the calories! The roll is large enough to feed a minor horde of sweet tooths.

SPONGE CAKE

4 eggs
200 g (7 oz) caster (superfine) sugar
120 g (4½ oz) plain (all-purpose) flour
1 teaspoon baking powder
30 g (1 oz) butter, melted
1 tablespoon warm water
1 teaspoon natural vanilla extract

FILLING

500 g (1 lb 2 oz) ricotta
50 g (1¾ oz) caster (superfine) sugar
40 g (1½ oz/¼ cup) almonds,
  toasted and chopped
40 g (1½ oz) dark chocolate,
  roughly chopped
2 tablespoons diced candied citrus
  peel (optional)
grated zest of ½ orange
1 teaspoon natural vanilla extract

1 sheet puff pastry (approximately
  30 × 35 cm/12 × 13¾ in)
125 ml (4 fl oz/½ cup) berry jam
2 tablespoons liqueur such as
  Prickly pear liqueur (page 217)
  or orange liqueur, or sweet vermouth
1 egg, lightly beaten
25 g (1 oz/¼ cup) flaked almonds
icing (confectioners') sugar,
  for dusting

HOW TO

Preheat the oven to 180°C (360°F) and line a rectangular Swiss roll (jelly roll) tin (about 25 × 35 cm/10 x 13¾ in) with baking paper. Beat the eggs in a mixing bowl for a few minutes until light and foamy. Rain in the sugar and beat for another 5 minutes – the eggs should become thick, creamy and roughly tripled in volume. Sift in the flour and baking powder and fold through gently. Add the butter, water and vanilla and fold gently until well combined. Pour the batter into the tin and bake for 20–25 minutes, or until a skewer comes out clean and the sponge is golden. Leave in the tin for 5 minutes before inverting onto a wire rack to cool.

Mix all the filling ingredients together in a bowl.

Trim the sponge down to 20 x 30 cm (8 × 12 in), sharing the trimmings with kids or keeping them for a small trifle.

Lay the sheet of pastry on a piece of baking paper. If the dimensions of the pastry are different to 30 × 35 cm (12 × 13¾ in), then roll it out to this size or trim down as needed. Spread the pastry with half the jam, leaving a 5 cm (2 in) border. Place the sponge cake on top of the jam, centred on the pastry. Sprinkle the sponge with the liqueur and spread with the remaining jam. Cover the sponge with the ricotta filling in an even layer. Roll up lengthways into a log, tucking in the pastry ends as you go.

Preheat the oven again to 180°C (360°F). Lift the log onto a baking tray using the baking paper. Brush the pastry with the beaten egg and sprinkle over the flaked almonds. Bake for 20 minutes, until the pastry is golden. Allow the sinizza to cool completely before dusting with icing sugar and slicing.

SFINEĠ TA' SAN ĠUŻEPP

SAINT JOSEPH'S FRITTERS WITH RICOTTA

PREPARATION: 30 MINUTES COOKING: 20 MINUTES

These sweet fritters made of choux pastry with a ricotta filling are also known as *zeppoli*. No doubt they are an evolution of Sicilian *sfinci*, and are delicious with coffee. Traditionally, they are prepared on 19 March for the feast of Saint Joseph. The savoury version of these fritters can be found on page 50.

CHOUX PASTRY

100 g (3½ oz) butter
120 ml (4 fl oz) water
120 ml (4 fl oz) milk
150 g (5½ oz/1 cup) plain
  (all-purpose) flour
1 pinch of salt
4 eggs, beaten

FILLING

500 g (1 lb 2 oz) ricotta
⅛ teaspoon natural vanilla extract
90 g (3 oz/¾ cup) icing
  (confectioners') sugar
40 g (1½ oz) diced candied
  citrus peel (optional)
40 g (1½ oz/¼ cup) almonds,
  roasted and chopped
50 g (1¾ oz) dark chocolate,
  chopped

1 litre (34 fl oz/4 cups) neutral oil
  for frying such as sunflower
  or canola
honey, to serve
chopped roasted almonds, to serve

HOW TO

Combine the butter, milk and water in a medium saucepan. Place over a medium heat and allow the butter to melt. Sift in the flour and stir vigorously with a wooden spoon, forming a paste. Add the salt and continue to cook over a low heat for 4 minutes, stirring constantly. You want to cook off the excess moisture, and allow a slight film to develop on the bottom of the pan. Scoop the dough into a large bowl, spreading it up the sides of the bowl to cool it down quickly.

When the dough is slightly warmer than room temperature, you can begin gradually beating in the egg with the wooden spoon. The dough is ready when glossy, and you can form a trench through the middle that holds its shape (you may not need all the egg).

Combine all the filling ingredients in a bowl and mix well.

Heat the oil in a heavy-based saucepan, and lower in a small piece of dough to check if it sizzles (the oil shouldn't be too hot or the fritters will brown too quickly). Use a metal spoon to scoop a heaped tablespoon of dough, then a second spoon to scrape the dough into an oval and carefully drop it into the oil. Continue to dollop more fritters into the oil. They should soon double in size. Flip the fritters regularly and cook until evenly golden (about 5 minutes). Drain on paper towel, and keep cooking the fritters in batches.

Use a serrated knife to make a cut lengthways in each fritter. Use a teaspoon to fill the fritters with some ricotta and place on a platter. Drizzle over some honey and sprinkle with almonds. Serve with the leftover ricotta and more almonds so people can spoon on extra as desired.

BAJTRA LIQUEUR

PRICKLY PEAR LIQUEUR

PREPARATION: 30 MINUTES + 10 DAYS STEEPING COOKING: 5 MINUTES

Thick stone boulder walls, hand built with incredible accuracy, divide properties all over Malta. It's here you will find endless prickly pear cactuses growing as windbreaks. The cactus, otherwise known by the Maltese as the berber fig, is an introduced species and thrives in Malta's climate. In autumn, the abundant fruit is used to make jam, syrup and liqueur – magnificent amber-pink. The pears need to be handled with caution because of their spines, which are both large and obvious, and tiny and hairlike. Handling and cooking the novel fruit is a lot of fun and the resulting flavour is unique. It reminds me of melon with a touch of artificial candy.

INGREDIENTS

1 kg (2 lb 3 oz) prickly pears
500 ml (17 fl oz/2 cups) vodka
700 ml (23½ fl oz) water
300 g (10½ oz) sugar

HOW TO

To protect your hands and fingers from the spines, it's best to handle the prickly pears by stabbing them with a fork, or covering your hand with a towel or a sturdy glove. Cut off the ends of the pears. Make 4 shallow cuts around each pear, lengthways through the skin from top to bottom. Carefully peel off the skin.

Drop the peeled pears into a large jar and add the vodka. Seal and store in a cool dark place for 10 days. The drink should develop an amber-red colour.

Heat the water and the sugar until the sugar dissolves, then set aside to cool. While the syrup is cooling, strain the vodka through a fine sieve and discard the fruit.

Mix the sugar syrup into the vodka. Pour into bottles and store in the refrigerator. Serve *bajtra* chilled in small glasses.

IMQARET

DATE-FILLED PASTRIES

PREPARATION: 35 MINUTES + 30 MINUTES CHILLING COOKING: 20 MINUTES

The name of these fried sweets translates as 'diamonds'. They are strikingly similar to *makrout* from North Africa, only those have the date filling encased in semolina pastry. *Imqaret* is one of the staple desserts of Malta, found in many homes and bakeries. They do little for the waistline – especially since it's become popular to serve them warm out of the fryer with vanilla ice cream! For the more health conscious, they can also be baked in the oven.

      The filling is easy to make and can be spiced as you like. If you can't find orange-blossom water, don't worry, as there is also fresh zest to impart flavour. I find the anise-scented pastry is what creates the magic here.

FILLING

200 g (7 oz) dates, pitted
  and chopped
grated zest and juice of ½ orange
½ teaspoon mixed
  (pumpkin pie) spice
1 tablespoon orange-blossom
  water (optional) or water

PASTRY

200 g (7 oz/1⅓ cups) plain
  (all-purpose) flour, plus extra
  for dusting
1 teaspoon ground aniseed
1 teaspoon baking powder
50 g (1¾ oz) butter
1 tablespoon icing
  (confectioners') sugar
1 egg, beaten

1 litre (34 fl oz/4 cups) neutral oil for
  frying such as sunflower or canola

HOW TO

Place all the filling ingredients in a saucepan and cook over a low heat, stirring occasionally, until the dates collapse and become a paste. Add some extra water during cooking if needed. Remove from the heat and leave to cool.

Combine the flour, aniseed and baking powder in a bowl. Add the butter and rub into the flour until the mixture resembles breadcrumbs or rough sand. Mix in the sugar. Add the egg and form into a dough. Shape into a disc, cover in plastic wrap and chill in the refrigerator for 30 minutes.

Roll the pastry on a lightly floured surface to a rectangle of 45 × 25 cm (18 × 10 in). Put the date paste in a line down the middle of the length of pastry. Brush a line of water above the date paste. Fold the pastry over the paste and press the pastry layers together where the water was brushed. Trim the excess pastry, creating a long strip of filled pastry with a seam. Cut the strip diagonally at 5 cm (2 in) intervals to make diamonds. (Don't throw out the excess pastry, as you could make an old treat called xkunvat: cut the pastry into strips and form shapes such as spirals and braids. Fry, and serve sprinkled with sugar or drizzled with honey.)

Heat the oil in a heavy-based saucepan, and lower a scrap of pastry into the oil to check if it sizzles. Carefully fry the date pastries in batches until golden brown. Remove with a slotted spoon and drain on paper towel. Serve with vanilla ice cream if desired.

Postcard #05

Wind your way down to the ferry.
Stretch the legs; spot her to the north.
A quick espresso on board.
Take in the salt spray outside.
Pass Comino with a quick glimpse of the lagoon.
Ascend the hill; the breads of Nadur await.
Dip toes in the sand at Ramla Bay.
Snorkel under the bouncing bright light
of the cliffs of Wied il-Għasri.
Sip on a Cisk lager; people-watch at St Francis Square.
Walk the Sanap Cliffs, pick some capers and soak in the view.
Toy with the vertigo, but be careful.
Head down to Xlendi, eat marinara by the marina while the water laps
and the sun drops over Phoenician wrecks.

MALTESE ORANGE TART

PREPARATION: 25 MINUTES + 30 MINUTES CHILLING COOKING: 45 MINUTES

The culinary bible *Larousse Gastronomique* cites 'sauce Maltaise' as a savoury preparation of hollandaise flavoured with blood orange. For a while, blood oranges were known as 'Maltese oranges' – so prized they were sent annually to Marie Antoinette in Versailles. This recipe captures the deliciousness of blood orange in a velvety curd, delivered in a delicate crust.

SWEET SHORTCRUST PASTRY

150 g (5½ oz/1 cup) plain
  (all-purpose) flour, plus extra
  for dusting
50 g (1¾ oz) icing
  (confectioners') sugar
75 g (2¾ oz) butter,
  chilled and diced
1 egg yolk
1 tablespoon iced water

BLOOD ORANGE CURD

3 large eggs
150 g (5½ oz) caster
  (superfine) sugar
grated zest of ½ blood orange,
  plus 100 ml (3½ fl oz) juice
1 tablespoon lemon juice
110 g (4 oz) butter,
  softened and diced
1 blood orange for garnish
  (sliced into thin discs)

HOW TO

Combine the flour, sugar and butter in a bowl and rub together with your fingertips until the mixture resembles breadcrumbs or rough sand. Add the egg yolk and water to form a dough. Shape into a ball, then flatten into a disc. Cover in plastic wrap and chill in the refrigerator for 30 minutes.

While the pastry is chilling, make the curd. Combine the eggs, sugar, zest and juices in a medium heatproof bowl and whisk together. Set the bowl above a saucepan of simmering water set over a low–medium heat. Cook, stirring often with a wooden spoon, for 15–20 minutes, or until the mixture thickens to a curd. It is ready when you are able to draw a line through the curd on the back of the spoon and it doesn't run. Stir in the butter until well blended and remove from the heat.

Preheat the oven to 170°C (340°F) and butter a 24 cm (9½ in) loose-based flan (tart) tin. Roll the pastry out on a floured surface until large enough to cover the tin. Line the tin with the pastry, pressing it into the sides. Trim the excess by rolling the pin across the top of the tin. Line with baking paper and fill with dried beans or rice (or weights) for blind baking. Bake for 15 minutes, then lift out the paper and contents and bake for 5 minutes more.

Allow the pastry shell to cool for at least 5 minutes, then fill with the curd. Bake for another 10 minutes. Leave the tart to cool, then chill in the refrigerator and serve cold.

For the blood orange garnish, slice the orange into thin discs. Place them on a wire rack and cook them in the oven for the last 5 minutes of the tart cooking. Leave them in the oven when you turn it off, with the door slightly ajar.

TORTA SAN MARTIN

SERVES 8

SAINT MARTIN'S FRUIT AND NUT CAKE

PREPARATION: 30 MINUTES + 1 HOUR SOAKING COOKING: 1 HOUR 15 MINUTES

Saint Martin's Day in November is a time when walnuts, almonds and dried figs are in abundance in Malta. In an ongoing custom, children are given bags of sweets, dried fruits and nuts similar to those in this cake, and there is a traditional rhyme honouring the foods and the saint. Many 'Saint Martin's' recipes involve these ingredients, with this cake one of the most popular. It's dense and protein-rich, and keeps well for days.

INGREDIENTS

120 g (4½ oz) dried figs, thinly sliced
60 ml (2 fl oz/¼ cup) dark rum
  or vermouth
150 g (5½ oz) soft, pitted dates,
  chopped
100 ml (3½ fl oz) water
80 g (2¾ oz) broken walnuts,
  plus 1 handful for garnish
100 g (3½ oz/⅔ cup) almonds,
  roasted and chopped,
  plus 1 handful for garnish
100 g (3½ oz) hazelnuts, roasted
  and chopped, plus 1 handful
  for garnish
1 large or 2 small apples, peeled
  and grated to give 170 g (6 oz)
80 g (2¾ oz) raisins, plus
  1 handful for garnish
grated zest of 1 medium lemon
200 g (7 oz/1⅓ cups) plain
  (all-purpose) flour
150 g (5½ oz) butter, softened
120 g (4½ oz) white sugar
4 large eggs
1 teaspoon baking powder
1 teaspoon ground cinnamon
1 teaspoon mixed spice
½ teaspoon ground cloves
4 tablespoons honey

HOW TO

Soak the figs in the rum or vermouth for 1 hour. Heat the dates and water in a saucepan over a medium heat. Once simmering, remove from the heat and mash to a paste with the back of a fork. Allow to cool.

Add the chopped nuts, apple, raisins, lemon zest and 2 tablespoons of the flour to the pan of date paste. Stir the mixture well.

In a large mixing bowl, whisk the butter and sugar until pale and creamy. Add the eggs one at a time and whisk until incorporated. Sift the remaining flour into a separate bowl and stir in the baking powder and spices. Fold this into the butter mixture. Now fold in the fruit and nuts.

When batter is combined, pour it into a floured cake tin. In a bowl, mix the garnish nuts and raisins with the honey using a spoon. Spoon mixture on to the cake before baking in oven. If the nuts start to brown too much add a layer of foil on top half way through cooking.

Preheat the oven to 165°C (330°F). Bake in the oven for 10 minutes, then reduce the temperature to 160°C (320°F) and bake for 55–60 minutes, or until a skewer or knife inserted in the middle tests clean. Allow to cool in the tin for 10 minutes, then remove to a wire rack. Allow to cool for at least an hour before serving.

IMBULJUTA TAL-QASTAN

CHESTNUT AND COCOA DRINK

PREPARATION: 10 MINUTES + OVERNIGHT SOAKING COOKING: 1 HOUR

This rich, warm drink is served at Christmas and New Year's Eve. Cocoa and chestnuts together with cloves, cinnamon, orange, star anise – can you imagine a more Christmassy concoction of smells? I can't; it fills the house! With no milk, the drink also happens to be vegan. If you feel the need for extra fortification, go ahead and add some coffee liqueur, whisky, rum or Baileys, as these all go exceptionally well with the drink.

INGREDIENTS

250 g (9 oz) dried peeled chestnuts, soaked overnight

zest of 2 large oranges – 1 finely grated, 1 cut off in strips

150 g (5½ oz) soft brown sugar

50 g (1¾ oz) unsweetened cocoa powder

1 cinnamon stick

1 star anise

6 cloves

1 teaspoon mixed (pumpkin pie) spice

1.5 litres (51 fl oz/6 cups) water

1 tablespoon cornflour (cornstarch) dissolved in 1½ tablespoons water

HOW TO

Drain the chestnuts and put them in a large saucepan. Add the grated orange zest (but not the strips) and remaining ingredients except the cornflour. Stir and bring to the boil, then simmer with the lid ajar for about 1 hour.

While the mixture continues to simmer, remove the cinnamon stick, star anise and any cloves you can find. Use the back of a large spoon to start crushing the chestnuts against the side of the pan, creating smaller pieces but leaving a chunky texture. Add the cornflour liquid and stir well. Simmer for a few more minutes to allow the drink to thicken. Serve in mugs or bowls garnished with the strips of orange zest.

PRINJOLATA

PREPARATION: 40 MINUTES + 3 HOURS CHILLING COOKING: 15 MINUTES

This easily distinguishable, decadent cake resembles some sort of crown jewel – a white dome studded with nuts and glacé cherries found all over Malta in the carnival before Lent. Having evolved over centuries, recipes vary greatly: the filling can include cake or whole or crushed biscuits, and the outside can be cream or meringue frosting. No matter the recipe, the cake must be tall in stature and contain pine nuts (*prinjol* means pine nut).

For the purest *prinjolata*, you can make your own biscuits or cake, but I find the effort unwarranted as they add little to the overall flavour, getting slightly lost in the glorious butter cream. Instead I use savoiardi biscuits (also known as lady or sponge fingers) for an easier but equally tasty cake.

FILLING

30 g (1 oz) pine nuts

100 g (3½ oz/1 cup) ground almonds

200 g (7 oz) butter, softened

3 tablespoons icing
  (confectioners') sugar

200 ml (7 fl oz) sweetened
  condensed milk

200 g (7 oz) savoiardi
  (lady fingers), halved

3 tablespoons vermouth

ITALIAN MERINGUE

150 g (5½ oz) sugar

65 ml (2¼ fl oz) water

2 large egg whites at room
  temperature

¼ teaspoon cream of tartar

TOPPING

50 g (1¾ oz) dark chocolate

20 g (¾ oz) pine nuts, toasted

20 g (¾ oz) pistachio nuts, toasted
  and roughly chopped

10 glacé cherries, halved

HOW TO

To make the filling, lightly toast the pine nuts in a dry frying pan. When golden, add the ground almonds to toast a little also. Set aside to cool.

Whisk the butter and icing sugar in a large bowl until pale and fluffy. Gradually whisk in the condensed milk. Add the savoiardi, vermouth and toasted nut mixture and stir everything together with a wooden spoon. It's okay if the biscuits break into smaller pieces. Scoop the filling into a tall bowl lined with plastic wrap (my bowl is 10 cm/4 in wide and 17 cm/6¾ in high). Press down on the filling, then chill in the refrigerator for at least 3 hours.

To make the meringue, combine the sugar and water in a small saucepan and heat gently, stirring until the sugar dissolves. Turn the heat up to medium–high and allow the syrup to come to a boil. In the meantime, combine the egg whites and cream of tartar in a heatproof bowl and beat to soft peaks. Once the syrup has reached 116°C (240°F) on a sugar thermometer (soft ball stage), slowly drizzle the hot syrup into the egg whites with the beaters running. Keep beating for several minutes, until the bottom of the bowl is no longer warm to touch. If convenient, this meringue can be made in advance and stored in the refrigerator.

Turn the chilled filling out onto a cake stand or serving plate. Peel off the plastic wrap. Use a spatula to spread the meringue all over the dome, smoothing the surface. Melt the chocolate in a heatproof bowl set over a saucepan of simmering water, or in a microwave. Transfer to a piping bag or use a spoon to drizzle lines of chocolate across the dome. Spin the cake 90 degrees and repeat the lines to create a crisscross effect. Decorate with the pine nuts, pistachio nuts and cherries. Allow the cake to come to room temperature for about 1 hour before slicing and serving.

Acknowledgements

Much love and respect to Linda, Max & Leon, thank you for your patience and understanding, giving me the opportunity to write this book.

To my family in Australia for encouraging my passion for food culture.

To the team at Hardie Grant Publishing, for believing in this book, Josephine Johansson for her splendid design and Rachel Pitts for her precise editing.

This book could not have been made without the help of many people who facilitated my research.

The Mattei family, especially Emma and Pippa. Phillip Spiteri, Liam Gauci, Dorianne Kurtcu Mifsud, Carina Dimech, Julia Busuttil Nishimura, Scott Duffy, Emily Caruana, Arthur Grima, Lawrence and David Bajada, Rikardu Zammit, Sam Cremona, George Zammit, Ryan Psailla, Alexandra Valetta, Darrell Azzopardi, Sharon Falzon, the Agius family at Tal-Karmnu farm, Kenneth Abela, Carmello Micallef and all the unnamed Maltese folk I accosted for conversations on food.

GRAZZI!

Index

Published in 2023 by Hardie Grant Books, an imprint of Hardie Grant Publishing

Hardie Grant Books (Melbourne)
Wurundjeri Country
Building 1, 658 Church Street
Richmond, Victoria 3121

Hardie Grant Books (London)
5th & 6th Floors
52–54 Southwark Street
London SE1 1UN

hardiegrant.com/au/books

Hardie Grant acknowledges the Traditional Owners of the country on which we work, the Wurundjeri people of the Kulin nation and the Gadigal people of the Eora nation, and recognises their continuing connection to the land, waters and culture. We pay our respects to their Elders past and present.

A catalogue record for this book is available from the National Library of Australia

NATIONAL LIBRARY OF AUSTRALIA

Malta
ISBN 978 1 74379 881 2

10 9 8 7 6 5 4 3 2

Publisher: Michael Harry
Project Editor: Antonietta Anello
Editor: Rachel Pitts
Design Manager: Kristin Thomas
Designer: Josephine Johansson
Production Manager: Todd Rechner
Production Coordinator: Jessica Harvie

Colour reproduction by Splitting Image Colour Studio
Printed in China by Leo Paper Products LTD.